Dot-Com to Dot-Bomb

Understanding the
Dot-Com Boom, Bust and Resurgence

Tapan Munroe

To my good friends Larry & Janet Sini —
all the best
Tapan Munroe
June 27, 2004

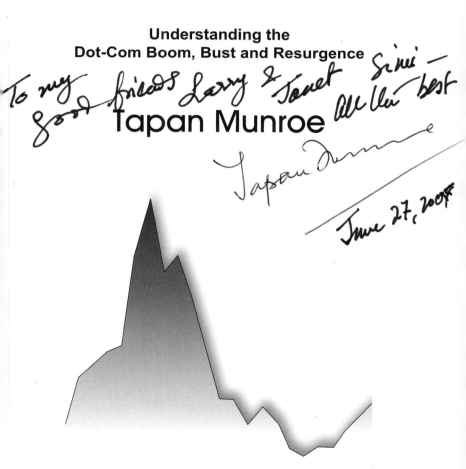

Moraga Press

DOT-COM TO DOT-BOMB
Copyright 2004 by Tapan Munroe

This book may be purchased for educational, business,
or sales promotional use. For information, please write:
Moraga Press
1480 Moraga Rd., Ste. I-237
Moraga, CA 94556
www.MoragaPress.com

Designed by Mark Westwind

ISBN 1-9755161-0-8
First edition published in May 2004.

Printed in the U.S. by
Galaxy Press
Concord, California

Table of Contents

Previous Books
by Tapan Munroe

Economic Imperialism
(with Kenneth Boulding)
University of Michigan Press

Public Power in California
(with Ted Bradshaw and Richard Lee)
Xlibris Corporation

Acknowledgements

The essays included in the Perspectives section of this book first appeared in my column – "Global Village" – published in the Contra Costa Times (a Knight Ridder newspaper). Thanks are due to Steve Trousdale, Contra Costa Times Business Editor and Craig Lazzeretti, Associate Business Editor for their guidance and support.

Mark Westwind, senior consultant with Munroe Consulting Inc., provided invaluable assistance with research, editing and book design. Maureen Dixon also helped with editing. Astrid Munroe provided much encouragement and guidance in the preparation of this book. Thanks are also due to Bob Meyer and his team at Galaxy Press for their valuable help in the production of this book.

This book is dedicated to my wife and best friend, Astrid Munroe.

Preface

This book is a result of several years of thinking and writing about the dot-com bubble. The nearly thirty month long boom to bust period of 1998-2001 parallels the speculative fever and mania and subsequent financial ruin experienced in previous world class bubbles such as the 17th century Tulip Mania in Western Europe, the 18th century South Sea Company bubble, and the Crash of 1929.

It is difficult to imagine that only a few years ago analysts, venture capitalists, and business leaders had the wild expectation that the melding of computers and communications technology would eliminate the business cycle and give us unending prosperity. Underlying this euphoric view of the future were unreal expectations involving the Internet. According to experts from technology centers as well as Wall Street the Internet was the greatest technological breakthrough since the wheel, the printing press, and even the telephone. Between mid-1998 and mid-1999 investors caught in the dot-com mania drove up the price of Internet related e-commerce stocks by 400%. But there was a fly in the ointment – the share price of most of the Internet-related firms could not be justified in light of their dismal financial performance. As a result, Internet-related stock prices collapsed. In just one week in March 2000, more than $2 trillion worth of equity wealth vanished into thin air.

The collapse of the dot-com bubble has had profound impact not only on investors who lost trillions but also on the thousands of workers who lost their jobs as their companies disappeared. It was one of the factors that triggered the recession of 2001 from which we have yet to fully recover.

This book is about understanding the dot-com bubble as well as the subsequent recovery of Internet-related businesses that appears to have started in 2003.

Section 1, the Prologue, provides an overview of what happened and why it happened.

Section 2, Perspectives, is a chronological compilation of columns I wrote for the *Contra Costa Times* (a Knight Ridder newspaper) between June 1999 and March 2004 tracing the anatomy of the rise and fall of the dot-coms.

Section 3, Epilogue, has two chapters, Lessons Learned and Resurgence. The former summarizes the lessons learned from the eighteen articles in section two. The latter deals with the revival of the dot-com industry as web-savvy businesses show the way to greater productivity and sustainable profitability.

Throughout this book, I have used the tech-heavy NASDAQ stock market index as a backdrop and surrogate for the dot-com boom to bust cycle. By the same token, the up-tick in the NASDAQ index since early 2003 serves as a symbol of the resurgence of the dot-coms and the technology sector in general.

I
Prologue

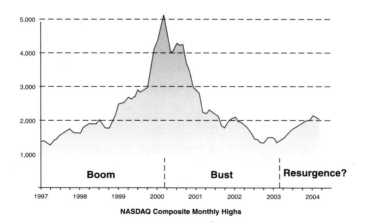

Boom   **Bust**   **Resurgence?**

NASDAQ Composite Monthly Highs

1

The Dot-com Gold Rush was on. But there were serious problems. The dot-com bubble follows the classic pattern of speculative bubbles that economies around the world have experienced for many centuries.

Understanding the Dot-com Bubble

It is difficult to imagine that only a few years ago a large number of analysts, investment bankers, and business leaders had the mushy expectation that the melding of computers and communications technology would eliminate the business cycle – giving us unending prosperity and even eliminating world hunger!

Underlying this euphoric view of the future were enormous expectations involving the Internet. According to many pundits from various technology centers in the United States and Wall Street, the Internet was the greatest technological breakthrough since the wheel, the printing press, or even the telephone. The financial markets, at least for a while, supported the spectacular promise of the Internet. Investors were willing to pay astronomical prices for shares in Internet-related companies. Between mid-1998 and mid-1999 investors (large and small, from individuals to mutual funds and pension funds) who were caught up in the dot-com mania drove up Internet stocks by more than 400 percent.[1]

The rush to cash in on the Dot-com Gold Rush was on. Entrepreneurs in most sectors of the economy jumped in to start online businesses with venture capital or angel capital, and many hoped that they would cash in once company shares were issued on the NASDAQ. On March 9, 2000, the NASDAQ closed over 5,000. The tech-heavy stock index had risen from 3,000 to 5,000 in four months.

But there were serious problems. The share price of a large number of Internet firms could not be justified in light of their financial performance, the soundness of their business propositions, and their spectacular "burn rate of money," a term that was coined in the Internet boom days. This was money that the startups had raised via venture capital financing or an initial public offering (IPO) of stocks in the NASDAQ and, amazingly enough, there was a race to see which startup could spend it fastest. These entrepreneurs felt they had to work in super-fast "Internet time," hiring staff, leasing office space, running full-page ads in the Wall Street Journal, and hosting golf tournaments or other high profile events to gain a "first-comer" advantage.

The enormous gap between valuation and performance led to a collapse of Internet stocks. Between March 10, 2000 and April 14, 2000, a five-week period, Akamai stock declined by 78 percent (from $296 to $65), Ariba went down by nearly 80 percent (from $395 to $62), Commerce One went down by nearly 74 percent (from $258 to $66), and VeriSign went down by nearly 60 percent (from $240 to $98). In just a week in March 2000, more than $2 trillion worth of equity wealth just evaporated.[2]

The dot-com boom-to-bomb cycle occurred approximately between October 1998 and April 2001 – a period of nearly 30 months. In this relatively short period, trillions of dollars were made and lost. The landscape of U.S. technology and its economic future were drastically altered. The golden dreams of many investors and young entrepreneurs were destroyed with the collapse of the NASDAQ and the disappearance of hundreds of dot-coms. How could such a financial earthquake happen in a country that is financially and technologically one of the savviest and most sophisticated in the world?

4

The answer is given very clearly in the book *Manias, Panics, and Crashes—A History of Financial Crises*, written by well known economic historian Charles Kindleberger first published in 1978:

> *As firms and households see others making profits from speculative purchases and resales, they tend to follow: "Monkey see, monkey do." In my talks about financial crisis over the last decade, I have polished one line that always gets a nervous laugh: "There is nothing so disturbing to one's well-being and judgment as to see a friend get rich." When the number of firms and households indulging in these practices grows large, bringing in segments of the population that are normally aloof from such ventures, speculation for profit leads away from normal, rational behavior to what has been described as "manias" or "bubbles." The word "mania" emphasizes irrationality; "bubble" foreshadows the bursting.[3]*

The dot-com bubble clearly follows the classic pattern of speculative bubbles that economies around the world have experienced for many centuries, including the Tulip Mania of 1634 in Holland, the South Sea Bubble of 1719 in London, and the Mississippi Bubble of 1720 in Paris. Charles Kindleberger's key point is that even in disparate places in the world and over centuries there are several common threads that link these financial disasters.

According to Kindelberger, bubbles occur after unexpected good news such as the promise of a new technology like the Internet. This results in new profit opportunities, which are seized with a great deal of zeal and hype. Early investors jump in on the opportunities while most investors wait and see. The early entrants make a bundle of money, and this gets the attention of those on the sidelines. A boom starts, prices increase rapidly, caution turns into greed, and the lure of easy money (and early retirement) draws a large number of investors into these highly risky enterprises. Prices rise further and even the most conservative and shy investors are drawn in, as they feel left out. The boom is now transformed into euphoria, and prices are decoupled from the realities of the financial and economic world. Eventually the bubble bursts as these prices are unsustainable. Prices drop rapidly, and companies go bankrupt. A large enough bubble causes an economic downturn.

The final question is: How could the spectacular Internet Bubble be sustained for 30 months? There are several factors that provided an unusually long life to this bubble. These include: a) theoretical legitimacy via the new paradigm: the "New Economy," b) enormous increases in media coverage and accompanying hype, and c) expansion of online trading, day traders, and 24/7 trading. A brief review of these issues is important in understanding the longevity as well as the driving forces of the Internet Bubble.

The "New Economy"

There are many recent books that deal with the fuzzy concept called the "New Economy." They range from *New Rules for a New Economy—Employment and Opportunity in Post Industrial America*, written by Stephen A. Herzenberg, John Alic, and Howard Wial (Cornell University Press, 1998), to *New Rules For the New Economy—10 Radical Strategies for a Connected World*, written by Kevin Kelly (Viking, 1998), and *The Digital Economy—Promise and Peril in the Age of Networked Intelligence* by Don Tapscott (McGraw Hill, 1996). Perhaps one of the more influential pieces written on the digital age and the New Economy came from the economics editor of *Business Week*, Michael Mandell, entitled *The Triumph of the New Economy*. The general theme of the spate of books and articles was that in the New Economy, the old rules of economics were no longer really relevant. From a macro economic perspective it was possible for the technology-led U.S. economy of the late 1990s to have low unemployment, rapid economic growth, high wages, and low inflation due to increases in productivity via massive investment in computers and information technology for more than a decade. This was a departure from decades long theorizing by economists about the near impossibility of all these good things coexisting at the same time.

Perhaps the most intriguing of the New Economy books is the one written by Kevin Kelly, an editor of the well-known digital age magazine *Wired*. There is much that is interesting and useful in terms of the nature of the digital revolution of the 1990s in this spirited and imaginative book. However, it really overreaches and stretches the imagination when it begins pontificating about the nature of the New Economy from an economic perspective. It is worth examining some paragraphs from the dust jacket of the book:

> *Forget Supply and Demand. Forget computers. Today communication, not computation, drives change. We are rushing into a world where connectivity is everything, and where old business know-how means nothing. In this new order, success flows primarily from understanding networks, and networks have their own rules.*

The problem with the paragraph above is that supply and demand has always been important and they will remain so in the future. Certainly communications and networks are very important, but we should not forget old business know-how. Revenues, costs, profits, market share, return on investment, and due diligence: they all matter.

Kelly's book lists ten fundamental rules of the New Economy. Here is one sample:

> *Plentitude, Not Scarcity —Industrial age wisdom says value comes from scarcity. But in a network economy, value comes from abundance. Consider the "fax effect." One fax machine is worth nothing. Even a small network of fax machines is valuable. But each machine added to a fax network increases the value of all the machines on the Network exponentially. The idea of plentitude is to create something that is connected to as many other products, services, and networks as possible.*

This is a provocative paragraph and it has a certain amount of shock value as there is a hint of denial of scarcity, as well as the implication that value is not really related to scarcity. Both of these suggestions fly in the face of everyday reality in business as well as in private life.

There are other attention grabbers sprinkled throughout this imaginative book such as:

> *Don't solve problems; pursue opportunities. (p. 146)*

> *Productivity however, is exactly the wrong thing to care about in the new economy. (p. 147)*

> *The problem with trying to measure productivity is that it measures only how well people can do the wrong jobs. Any jobs that can be measured for productivity probably should be eliminated from the list of jobs that people do. (p. 148)*

The problem with these statements is that they suggest that the era of the Internet brings with it a new system of economics where concepts of fundamental importance in business and economics such as productivity, hence efficiency, are no longer relevant because productivity increases will be automatic. All workers have to do is the "right thing," which, in Old Economy businesses, is usually in the province of a company's top executives. In the New Economy, doing the "right thing" all the time becomes the province of most workers. It is an attractive idea, but how realistic is it? It is an extraordinary challenge that the "New Economy" imposes on workers in digital age businesses—one that is very difficult, if not impossible to meet.

These and other New Economy theorists provided a seductive basis for Wall Street as well as Main Street to continue investing in enormously over-priced stocks by giving the Internet revolution the New Economy ideology and thus legitimacy. Investors thought it also meant a new arena for investing where the "old" guidelines such as diversification, studying a company's fundamentals to see if it has intrinsic value, and a wariness of stocks selling at 50 to 100 times earnings or more, no longer held.

The rising legitimacy of the New Economy with its underlying message of "throw away the old business rules" emboldened people in diverse walks of life with little or no business experience (or knowledge) to Web-based businesses. They were no longer burdened by the usual constraint of starting a business—a "realistic chance of making money." The sky was the limit. Why not start Web-based businesses for dog or cat owners? Why not a business for perfume lovers? Why not a business for home delivery, no matter how small the delivery is? Once a spate of favorable articles and TV interviews came out, money became available and another e-business was spawned—the company was well on its way to an IPO.

Increase in Media Coverage

The first all-news TV station, CNN, was established in 1980. The Financial News Network (FNN) in 1983, which was bought out by CNBC in 1991, followed it. Bloomberg Television came next – the result was continuous business news coverage that was mostly devoted to the stock market. Undoubtedly this boosted the demand for stocks just as advertisement boosts sales of things we can consume.[4]

People could not get enough news about the latest happenings related to their stocks. The financial networks treated the happenings in the market as recreational events such as baseball and football. Even on days when things were not going well in the market the commentators and anchor people were upbeat and enthusiastic. In effect the financial networks became market boosters even though that was not their formal intent.

New Economy financial magazines such as *Wired, Fast Company, The Industry Standard, Upside, Red Herring,* and *Business 2.0* did their part in enhancing the legitimacy of the notion of the New Economy by becoming the voice of the new era of prosperity via investments in Internet-related stocks. The stage was set for the stock market boom and bust of 1998–2000. Today, after the bust, only three of the six magazines, *Fast Company, Wired,* and *Business 2.0* are still around. John Cassidy correctly points out in his book that the rapid appearance of many magazines focused on the same business is one symptom of a bubble reaching its peak.[5] This was the case during the British Railroad Mania of the 1840s. In this period, the railway press included 14 new weekly papers and two new daily papers with names such as *The Railway Review, The Railway World, The Rail-*

way Examiner, and so on. Most of these publications vanished with the crash in 1847.

To a significant degree, the Internet Boom was created and sustained by the media, and in turn journalists, writers, and TV commentators became players in many Internet-based media companies in addition to their role as media professionals.

Expansion of Trading

The volume of stock trading increased dramatically between 1982 and 1999 with the New York Stock Exchange "turnover rate" (ratio of total shares sold to total number of shares during a year) increased from 42 percent to 78 percent. In the case of the NASDAQ, the same ratio increased from 88 percent in 1990 to 221 percent in 1999. This was a result of technological (online trading) and organizational changes that included the appearance of discount brokers and day traders, amateur investors who were using the same execution systems as professionals.[6] This rapid escalation in the market was nothing compared to what happened after 1997.

The spectacular rise of the stock market, particularly the tech-heavy NASDAQ, between 1997 and 1999 coincides with the rise in online trading as well as the rise in Internet-based around-the-clock stock market information. In 1997, there were 3.7 million online accounts and by 1999 there were a staggering 9.7 million.[7]

People were hooked on the "24 hours a day 7 days a week" stock market information just as in earlier periods they were hooked on baseball and football programs. There was almost a recreational aspect to knowing about goings on in Wall Street and knowing about all the fortunes that were being made on various high tech stocks.

11

For many people buying and selling stocks became an addiction. This undoubtedly gave rise to speculation and a "get rich quick" mentality that enhanced the market boom, and ultimately, the bust.

All of these factors coalesced to bring the largest bubble any of us have seen in our lifetime – which, in turn, led to a tremendous disappointment as the bubble burst and trillions of dollars of wealth simply evaporated.

Many companies learned vital lessons during this time, however, and Internet-related businesses were spawned that used the Internet wisely, as a tool, not as an end product. There were also numerous businesses, such as eBay and Google, that had been making wise use of the Internet all along, and they have continued to grow and prosper.

Footnotes

1   Anthony B. Perkins, and Michael C. Perkins, *The Internet Bubble,* Harper Business, 1999, p. 3

2   John Cassidy, *Dot.Con The Greatest Story Ever Sold,* HarperCollins, 2002, p. 293

3   C. P. Kindleberger, *Manias, Panics, and Crashes – A History of Financial Crises,* Basic Books, 1989, pp. 19–20

4   Robert J. Schiller, *Irrational Exuberance,* Princeton University Press, 2000, p. 29

5   John Cassidy, op. cit., p. 177

6   Robert Schilling, op. cit., p. 39

7   Securities and Exchange Commission, *Special Study: Online Brokerage – Keeping Apace of Cyberspace,* 1999, http://www.sec.gov/pdf/cybtrend.pdf

II
Perspectives

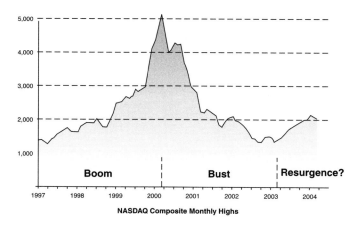

NASDAQ Composite Monthly Highs

Dot-com to Dot-Bomb

Chronology of Columns by Tapan Munroe
June 1999 to March 2004

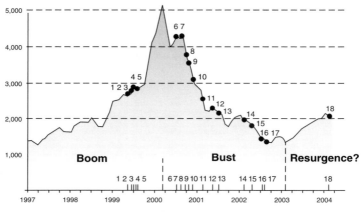

NASDAQ Composite Monthly Highs

No.	Date	Column Title
1	June 1999	What's New in the New Economy?
2	July 1999	New Rules on the Cost of Information
3	July 1999	Privacy In the New Economy
4	July 1999	The New Economy Threatens Some Industries
5	Aug. 1999	How the New Economy Generated New Wealth
6	July 2000	E-tailing's Shakeout May Be Good
7	Aug. 2000	Reality Takes Wind Out of Online Sales
8	Sept. 2000	E-Commerce Still Subject to "Old" Economic Principles
9	Oct. 2000	Is the New Economy for Real?
10	Nov. 2000	Despite the Web, Location Matters
11	Feb. 2001	The Internet is no Panacea for Business
12	May 2001	Tulips, Manias and Bubbles
13	July 2001	Making E-tailing Work
14	Feb. 2002	Don't Judge the Net on Financial Success Alone
15	Apr. 2002	The New Economy Gets a Bad Name
16	July 2002	Silicon Valley After the Dot-com Bomb
17	July 2002	If You Build It, They May Not Come
18	Mar. 2004	"Smart" Internet Promises Bright Future for High-Tech

Points in Time

In this section, I have collected eighteen articles relating to the rise and fall of the Internet economy that I wrote as a columnist for the *Contra Costa Times*, a Knight Ridder newspaper, between June 1999 and March 2004. The chart to the left displays these articles chronologically with the NASDAQ indicator as a backdrop symbolizing the rise and collapse of the dot-com bubble between 1994 and 2002. It is interesting to note that in this period I was somewhat ahead of the curve in anticipating the developments of the boom-bust cycle. These short chapters track the boom, bust and resurgence as they happened or as I anticipated the events.

E-commerce is now making resurgence, with the Internet recognized and utilized for what it does best. These companies have also learned that the old economic principles still apply, even in the "New Economy." The Internet is still alive and well, and enhancing our businesses as well as our personal lives. The companies that will prosper using the Internet will be the ones that can successfully meld old economic common sense with this powerful new technology.

1

What's New
in the New Economy?

Perspective: June 1999 ★

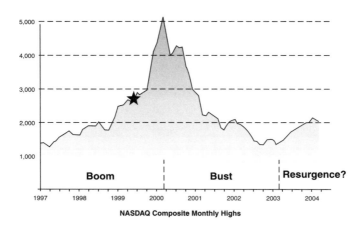

NASDAQ Composite Monthly Highs

Beyond enormous technological and structural changes, what's new about the New Economy?
Not much! Most of us still work. We buy and worry about costs. We sell and worry about revenue and expenses.

1

Software billionaire Bill Gates' testimony at the recently concluded National Summit on High Technology in Washington D.C. attracted twice the audience as that of Federal Reserve Chairman Alan Greenspan. Gates' vision of a world where consumers manage their lives from a "digital dashboard" as a result of the rapid convergence of the Internet, telecommunications, computers, and consumer electronics is provocative and engaging. It was not his spellbinding oratory that packed the hearing room in the nation's capital but his vision and the importance of the subject matter. The summit turned out to be a Washington D.C. version of a seminar on the importance of the "New Economy."

What is the New Economy? How different is it from the Old Economy? Perhaps the authorship of the term "New Economy" can be attributed to Canadian economist Nuala Beck due to her contributions on the subject in her 1992 book *Shifting Gears: Thriving in the New Economy.* Her thesis is that in the last two decades we have witnessed a steady transition from an economy that has been powered by inexpensive fossil fuels to one powered by inexpensive semiconductors. The so-called "Old Economy," the one most of us are familiar with, is driven by four key industries — automobiles, machine tools, housing, and retailing. In contrast, the key industries of the New Economy include semiconductors, computers, software, the Internet, telecommunications, and biotechnology.

Long-Term Trends

Some of the important manifestations of the New Economy are highlighted in several long-term structural trends:

- More people today work in the computer hardware, software, and services industries than in the steel, auto, mining, and petroleum industries.
- Biotechnology employs more people than the machine tools industry.
- Nearly 80 percent of all jobs today do not involve making things but rather serving businesses or people and creating and processing information.
- Nearly 350,000 fast-growing "gazelle" firms—businesses that double their sales every four years, are creating 75 percent of all new jobs.
- More than 30 percent of all jobs are in a state of "churn"—either being created or dying as a result of new technology or competition.

At the end of 1998 the market value of IBM was twice the combined market value of Ford, GM, and Boeing; the market value of Microsoft, the world's highest valued company, was three times the combined market value of Ford and GM; and Intel's market value was 50 times greater than that of Nucor, the highest valued steel company.

The New Economy is more about "soft" and intangible things such as information, intellectual capital, relationships, communications, and networks, and less about "hard" and tangible things such as steel, oil, and lumber. This, of course, does not imply that "hard" things are unnecessary. The point is that hard things are increasingly built around the "soft" core—factories are run on computer commands, automobiles follow network instructions to manage congestion, and homes become smarter with embedded computer chips that control their physical environment, security, and entertainment.

Communication, Not Computers

The New Economy is not just about computers. All the things that computers can do as stand-alone machines have been attained in the last 20 years—massive data crunching, data warehousing, and word processing, thereby increasing our productivity and quickening our lives considerably. The New Economy from here on will be centered more on communication—with computer and telecommunications devices providing nearly instantaneous computation and connection.

The rise of the Internet has ushered in the next logical phase of the New Economy. What it does is provide con-

B2C E-Commerce Growth: The Sky's the Limit!

Survey of Online Sales Projections
($ billions worldwide)

—✗— Forrester Research
—✗— Gartner Research
—△— Jupiter Research
—□— eMarketer
—○— Yankee Group

Early on, projections for business-to-consumer (B2C) e-commerce sales growth looked fantastic but consumer concerns over security and fulfillment problems hindered such a rapid acceptance of on-line purchasing.
Source: American Marketing Association, 2001

nectivity the other prime feature of the New Economy. The penetration rate of the Net has been spectacular. Nearly 170 million people around the world today obtain information, create products, shop, converse, and on occasion even propose marriage via the Web. A mind-numbing 3.5 billion e-mail messages pass through the Net every day. In 1999 U.S. businesses are expected to spend more than $80 billion on the Internet. By 2001 that is expected to nearly double. This is indeed impressive if we consider that only six years ago the Internet was just a technical novelty—a communications link between a select group of scientists and universities.

Business-to-Business

The real economic potential of the Internet lies in business-to-business e-commerce. One estimate suggests that in 1998 businessees purchased nearly $43 billion worth of products and services over the Net compared to only $8 billion by consumers. It is expected that in the next five years the majority of e-commerce will be between businesses.

The enormous creation of wealth through the spectacular rise of the Dow and the NASDAQ and the churn we experienced in the last decade has been exhilarating as well as nerve-racking. But beyond enormous technological and structural changes what is new about the New Economy? From a fundamental economic perspective, the answer is—not much. Most of us still work to make a living. We buy and worry about costs. We sell and worry about revenue and expenses. We still have to make choices, as there is not an unlimited supply of all desirable things, including our talent and abilities. So not much has really changed—the principles we learned in Economics 101 classes still apply.

2

New Rules on the Cost of Information

Perspective: July 1999 ★

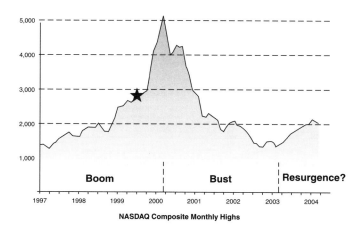

NASDAQ Composite Monthly Highs

Knowledge and information have always been important. But in the New Economy, they reign supreme. With the cost of creating information high and the cost of reproducing information low, businesses face a serious challenge of protecting "intellectual property."

2

There have been enormous technological and structural transformations in our economy as well as in the way business is done that are based on changes in the cost of creating and selling information. What are they?

Knowledge and information have always been important. But in the New Economy they reign supreme. There are different types of values that we obtain from information – business value, entertainment value, social value, environmental value – and we are willing to pay for the information based on our priorities. For success in the New Economy, we must remember that creating information is expensive, but reproducing it is not. Thus, publishing a book costs thousands of dollars but reprinting it costs only a few. The cost of producing the latest "*Star Wars*" movie ran into millions, but we will be able to buy or rent it in our local video store for a few dollars. What is the implication of this?

New Pricing Rules

Simple mark-up pricing, adding a flat percentage to the unit cost, is no longer the rule. Things need to be priced on the basis of their value to customers and not just by production cost. For example, Web-based investment services charge a fixed fee, let us say $10 a month, and provide personal stock portfolio analysis using day-old market numbers. The same service with real-time prices may cost $60 a month. The strategy of information businesses today is to sell different versions of the same product for different prices depending on their value to customers.

With the cost of creating information high and the cost of reproducing information low, businesses face a serious challenge of protecting intellectual property – the core asset of a business in the New Economy. It is a complicated and a difficult challenge, due to the spectacular success of the Internet and developments in digital technology.

The Internet, in a sense, has become a free-for-all global copy machine. Valuable information can be accessed from anywhere at any time. It can also be easily duplicated and communicated via the Internet because of negligible reproduction and distribution costs. There's always the danger of cheap copies replacing the original product, thereby forcing the legitimate company out of business.

New Model

Today's successful businesses are following a strategy that is different from the obvious one of going on a protective binge. They are using the low distribution cost implicit in digital technology to combat pilfering of information. They are actually giving away samples of information in order to entice customers to browse and eventually purchase the product.

Very few people want to read an entire book online; it is uncomfortable to do so visually and ergonomically. Therefore, a lot of material can be placed online without much fear of losing sales of hard-copy versions. The experiences of the National Academy of Science Press and the Massachusetts Institute of Technology (MIT) Press suggest that making some of the text available online has more than doubled sales. One secret of success: easy to browse, but difficult to print.

With an abundance of information and relatively easy access, another challenge of the New Economy is information overload. Information-content businesses provide useful data for customers, often by sorting it out or presenting it in a user-friendly form. It is no surprise that the most desirable Web sites are the ones linked to search engines.

The challenge of creating successful Web sites has to do with drawing repeat attention. Amazon.com has entered into an agreement with America Online to increase its reach via millions of AOL customers. Let us not forget that commercials support TV broadcasting and that newspapers and magazines are mostly supported by advertisements. The same principle applies to e-commerce – ads on Web sites are potentially a major source of revenue.

A key advantage of Web-based advertising is that it can offer one-on-one marketing; it can obtain data on many customers and rapidly produce tailor-made content as well as advertisements. A company taking advantage of this niche is Hotmail. It provides free e-mail service to anyone who will respond to a personal questionnaire. This allows the company to provide customized ads.

One of the most important imperatives of the New Economy is that these new businesses are information businesses. Even industries that are not typically classified as information businesses have enormous information content. More than one-third of our $300 billion in health care costs, for instance, is taken up in developing, storing and processing information on patients and insurance claims. Failure to realize this may make the difference between survival and oblivion.

The recent book *Information Rules* cites the well-known case of Encyclopedia Britannica, which lost most of its market share to Encarta and other CD ROM-based encyclopedias.

Britannica's management overlooked the fact that the largest chunk of its cost was not editorial content—only 5 percent—but its sales force. Britannica depended on a different rule: door-to-door sales, not digital technology.

Today, many large industries, including insurance, travel, automotive, and real estate, still depend on the intensive personal selling approach. The lesson from the Britannica case is a critical reminder for them: Information is a core asset of their business, so they must use the most efficient path for collecting, storing, and communicating information. Of course, that means the Internet.

3

Privacy in the New Economy

Perspective: July 1999 ★

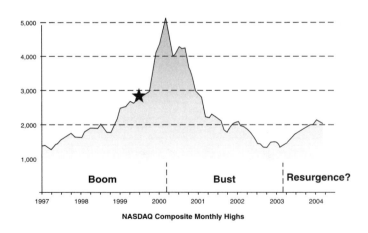

NASDAQ Composite Monthly Highs

In today's wired world, the information we provide about ourselves is recorded, stored, and sold every day without our knowledge. Preventing illegal and unethical use of information will always remain a struggle—each new move to protect private information will be countered by efforts to uncover it.

3

As we move deeper into the territory of the New Economy we face an enormous challenge in maintaining our personal and financial privacy.

We enjoy the New Economy's impressive benefits that include: greater productivity, hence lower inflation, spectacular entertainment, great advances in health care, improvements in crime detection, better government and private services, easier shopping, and enormous advances in communications. But many believe these benefits come with a huge personal price tag – loss of privacy.

In today's wired world, the information we provide about ourselves is recorded, stored, and sold every day without our knowledge. The use of a credit or a bank debit card, most financial transactions, loan and insurance applications, telephone calls, and use of the Internet and electronic tollbooths provides a constant flow of data about us. The buying and selling of all types of consumer information is a huge growth industry. As I write, there is even a computer hacker's convention put on by DEF CON taking place in Las Vegas.

A recent poll conducted by Peter D. Hart Research Associates concludes that 80 percent of adults surveyed express concern that computers and the Internet are a major source of loss of privacy. The poll further concludes that the top seven causes of loss of privacy in order of significance are: 1) credit bureaus, 2) business-to-business information sales,

31

3) states selling driver's license lists, 4) health companies sharing medical records, 5) use of social security numbers for identification purposes, 6) hidden cameras at work, and 7) employers monitoring phone calls.

But businesses are not just interested in consumers. They are also interested in knowing what their employees are doing in the workplace. A survey by the American Management Association in 1997 concluded that more than 60 percent of the large firms surveyed were monitoring employees' e-mail and telephone conversations.

It is not just businesses that are interested in keeping track of their customers and employees. Governments are also keenly interested in using New Economy technologies to improve the "public good" they provide. Government objectives range from improving health care delivery to fighting crime. Today the intelligence organizations of several English-speaking western nations including the U.S., U.K., and Canada monitor all international satellite telecommunication messages. An international DNA database of convicted criminals also exists.

The implications of what I have described are not that we should stop giving our telephone numbers to legitimate parties, or filling out forms in doctors' offices or mortgage loan applications, or using credit cards. Rejecting these day-to-day processes would be like courting "voluntary primitivism." It would mean denying the basic realities of life and missing out on the benefits that the New Economy bestows on us. For every advance and major transition we have made in human history there have been new obstacles and challenges. The current transition to the New Economy is no exception. There are solutions to the privacy problem! What are they? How effective are they?

The first is a legal solution. In the 1970s consumer credit laws were passed that gave us the right to look into our credit records and request corrections. A recent European Union (EU) version of the law is even stricter. It requires an individual's consent before an agency can process or store his or her information. The EU has mandated prevention of data export to countries that do not have similar laws. Many think that such a law is extreme and will hamper the development of e-commerce in Europe and end Europe's participation in the New Economy. It is unlikely that we will have such legislation passed in the U.S. in the foreseeable future.

The second solution is technological. Recently the World Wide Web Consortium (known as W3C) has proposed a solution that gives users more control over how personal information is used. The new protocol (a computer language that allows communication between networks), called P3P, allows clients to indicate desired levels of privacy. This technology looks promising, and I would not be surprised to see Microsoft or one of its competitors beginning to offer such a product this year.

The third is a market-based solution. With rising concerns about privacy on the Internet, new businesses, known as "re-mailers," have surfaced that forward e-mail minus any revealing identification of the sender. I wonder if such a service will provide as much privacy as the low-tech letter via the post office. Another emerging business may be a service that maintains consumers' privacy in transactions with businesses. This type of company can only be successful if consumers funnel all their transactions via a few companies.

Much as I prefer market solutions, at this point they appear to be inadequate in light of the enormous onslaught on our privacy from public as well as private sources. With enormous growth in information technology, the desire for information is insatiable. The demand for confidential information is particularly high. This is so because possessing it is profitable, and its availability is enormously beneficial to all of us, both socially and economically. The challenge is to prevent snooping. Preventing illegal and unethical use of information will always remain a struggle—each new move to protect private information will be countered by efforts to uncover it.

I see a future in which the "information protection" industry continues to be a growth industry. Technological and market based innovations and legal remedies will continue to evolve, with marginal gains on the side of privacy. I think we have always had less privacy than we thought we had. The chances are that in the future we will have even less!

4

The New Economy
Threatens Some Industries

Perspective: July 1999 ★

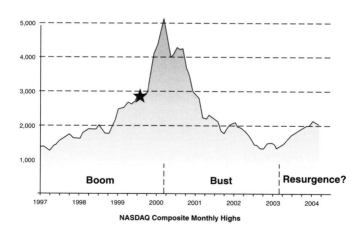

NASDAQ Composite Monthly Highs

The days of the "cowboy economy" are over as we enter the world of e-business – the world of connectivity. A new business model is emerging that suggests very few businesses can survive by remaining "lone rangers."

4

While most of our day-to-day Internet-related attention has been focused on the glamorous (shopping for books, CDs, art), the sleazy (pornography), and the scary (extremist babble), there is a less noticed but profound change taking place that is sure to change the landscape of American business. The Internet is changing the way business is done! Traditional product distribution channels are disappearing, the boundaries between sellers and buyers are blurring, and most importantly a new business model is emerging that suggests that very few businesses can survive by remaining "lone rangers." The days of the "cowboy economy" are over as we enter the world of e-business—the world of "connectivity."

Which well-established businesses are at risk in the New Economy? What do they have to do if they are to survive and prosper into the 21st century? I will discuss two among many industries that are likely to be most impacted by the Internet juggernaut. There are others, but limitations of space prohibit me from discussing them.

Insurance Agencies

The $670 billion U.S. insurance industry has been slow in moving into online sales via the Internet relative to brokerages and banks. A recent study by Forrester Research suggests that nearly 40 percent of insurance companies surveyed either did not think that the Internet was an important avenue for sales or did not have any plans for using the

Web. Even more discouraging is the fact that nearly a third of the insurance companies did not have any plans for using the Web.

The main reason why many insurance companies have not embraced the Net is the fear of antagonizing insurance agents. Increasingly agents fear "disintermediation"—the companies cutting them out of the loop. Agents have been a key to this business for selling policies as well as renewals. The personal relationship between agent and customer has been the cornerstone of the business, and communicating complex policy details to customers via agents has been the standard practice.

The emerging model of insurance businesses that are Web savvy is one where the business provides information and comparison-shopping via the Net, and the agents provide the final sale. A small number of sites are offering direct online sign up for policies. An example of this would be Intuit Insurance Services where customers can pay for policies online via their credit cards. Some types of policies such as auto insurance are obvious candidates for online sales. Things become more complex when dealing with health and life policies and many customers prefer to talk to a person rather than do business via the Web.

A likely scenario for the industry is that we will be seeing more direct sales of policies via the Internet. The role for insurance agents then becomes one of answering customer questions and maintaining long-term relationships for policy servicing and renewal. Another risk the insurance companies face is competition from banks and brokerages. Within a few years the majority of banks and brokerages will be selling insurance policies via their online services. "One stop shopping" via the Web will be the dominant theme in financial and risk management businesses. Insurance agents will have to adjust and add value to this new architecture of business or invite extinction like the Dodo bird!

Travel Agents

The $130 billion U.S. travel agency business is facing tough times. Competition from Internet-based discount airfare sites such as Priceline.com as well as several Web-based travel businesses including Travelocity and Expedia (Microsoft) is cutting into sales. Even the few Web-based travel agents are having a tough time due to increasingly stringent online commission policies of the airlines and direct competition from aggressive sites operated by airlines such as United, American, Delta, and US Airways.

The biggest hit on the travel agency business came from a general cutback in ticket sales commissions. In 1995, a cap of $50 was imposed on the existing 10 percent commission. This was further reduced to 8 percent by 1997. This reduction has hurt travel agency revenues badly as most of their revenues originate from ticketing commissions. It is very likely that hotel and resort commissions for travel agents will follow the same path as airlines.

Today, successful travel agents provide extraordinary customer service while carving out specific niches that respond to special travel itineraries, vacation and cruise packages, adventure travel, and eco-tourism. In addition they provide Net-based services as an option. To remain viable, travel agents will have to pursue the "high-tech, high touch" route that banks now use that allows customers to choose when they want personal contact and when they want their services online. Gone are the days when a travel agent could sell airline tickets and receive as much as a 10 percent commission on the value of the ticket. In the near future, creativity, staying current with technology, and partnering with the customer will be critical to a travel agent's survival. Other industries that are bound to change dramatically in the age of the Internet include auto dealerships, newspapers, food and beverage, drugstores, office supplies, utilities, and chemicals, among others. In a sense, the Internet is profoundly changing most industries. It is perhaps the single most important technology causing sweeping changes in the way we do business and the way we live since the advent of electricity. Denying its importance and significance is tantamount to joining the Luddites.

5

How the
New Economy
Generated New Wealth

Perspective: August 1999 ★

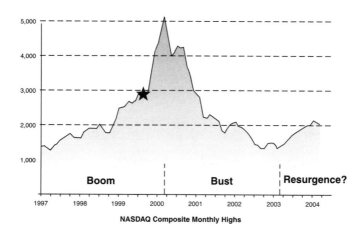

NASDAQ Composite Monthly Highs

The most spectacular
and fastest rise to riches
involves the "dot-com"
and Internet billionaires.
Sixty-four new millionaires
are created every day
in the San Francisco
Bay Area, but there
are challenges amid
this unprecedented
prosperity.

5

Without any doubt America has more rich people than any other country. According to Forbes, at the beginning of 1999 there were more than 460 billionaires worldwide, with more than 200 of those living in the United States.

Seven of the world's Top 10 billionaires are from the United States. Most of the new "super-rich" work, and they are getting richer faster than ever. Most of their wealth is on paper, thanks to the spectacular rise of the stock market. The new rich are younger. They certainly can afford "Arabian Nights" palaces, but very few have them. They are too busy starting their next company or initiating an IPO.

Today there are only a handful of world figures that can be defined as non-working rich. They are usually royalty or dictators, ranging from the Sultan of Brunei ($30 billion) to Queen Elizabeth II ($2 billion). Overwhelmingly the majority of their wealth originates from oil, gas, and large land holdings.

Another category of non-working rich includes coupon clippers—those who live off dividends from passive stock-holdings. This is a dwindling list. The richest people in this category are mostly from Europe, and their families maintain very low profiles. Most of us have not heard of the Hoffman and Sacher families of Switzerland who own a large chunk of Roche pharmaceuticals, or the Quandt family of Germany who owns nearly 50 percent of BMW.

New Economy Industries

Most of the new super-rich originate in the New Economy industries such as software, telecommunications, and the Internet. Of the Top 10 richest persons in the world, three are from Microsoft – Bill Gates (worth $90 billion to $100 billion depending on the state of the stock market), Paul Allen ($30 billion), and Steven Ballmer ($19.5 billion) – and one from Dell Computer, Michael Dell ($16.5 billion).

Tracing Bill Gates' rise to the top of the billionaires list is illustrative of the importance of the information economy as well as the phenomenal rise of the stock market in wealth building. Between 1990 and 1999 the Dow rose from 3,000 to more than 11,000. Bill Gates first appears in the Top 10

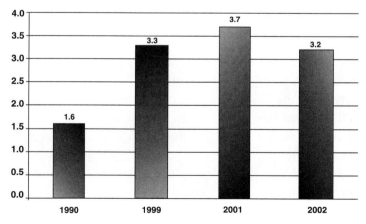

New Economy Wealth Generation and Destruction
Number of U.S. Millionaires (millions)

The number of wealthy Americans rose dramatically in the late 1990s, peaking with the crest of the NASDAQ in 2001. The number of millionaires declined rapidly with the steep fall in the NASDAQ after 2001. Source: Global Internet Marketing News, Dec. 1999, St. Petersburg Times, Sept. 2002 list in 1992 as the seventh richest person in the world, in 1996 he was ranked second, and he has been Number 1 since 1997. What is really astounding is that his net worth jumped by nearly 76 percent between 1998 and 1999.

The most spectacular and fastest rise to riches involves the dot-com or Internet billionaires. Take the case of 43 year-old Jay Walker of Priceline.com, who launched the Internet auction company in March 1999 with $27 million. His net worth today is more than $10 billion. Thirty-five year-old Jeff Bezos of Amazon.com launched the Internet book sales company a few years ago. The stock price is up more than 5,000 percent, and his personal net worth is more than $10 billion today, give or take a few hundred million depending on the mood of the market on a given day. Then there is the story of Pierre Omidyar, 31, who took eBay public in September 1998 at a split-adjusted $6 a share, with the share price rising to a split-adjusted $234 earlier in the year. His net worth today is approximately $8 billion.

Flush with Billionaires

The San Francisco Bay Area is a region flush with billionaires, including Larry Ellison of Oracle, Omidyar and Jeffrey Skoll of eBay, Jerry Yang and David Filo, founders of Yahoo!, and Charles Schwab. These are tremendous business success stories for this region, one of the leading "New Economy" regions of the world.

However, just talking about the billionaires does not give us a complete picture. Anecdotal estimates suggest that nearly 64 new millionaires are created every day in the Bay Area, nearly all of them in knowledge- and information-based industries. This is wealth creation at very impressive level. But there are challenges amid this unprecedented prosperity.

These challenges are:

- People are becoming rich very fast, but do they have the time and energy to enjoy their affluence? I hear more and more talk about "sudden wealth syndrome," a phenomenon that spills over occasionally into poor taste or lifestyle decisions.
- Enormous increases in home prices in areas such as San Francisco and Silicon Valley are pricing out middle-class home buyers.
- The word "millionaire" has lost its earlier meaning. A decent home in the Bay area costs nearly $500,000, and an appropriate SUV is priced at $35,000. Dinner for two at a good restaurant in the Bay Area costs more than $100.
- Inequality in the Bay Area has not really diminished despite enormous wealth creation. We have new challenges such as the "digital divide" where access to the Internet and other information technologies is a continuing problem for many in the region.

These issues are challenging and important for us to face. But before we begin to get depressed about some of these trends, let us not forget that we have an enormous wealth-creating machine and enormous talent right here in the Bay Area. If we cannot deal with these problems here, where in the world would we go to solve them?

6

E-tailing's Shakeout May Be Good

Perspective: July 2000 ★

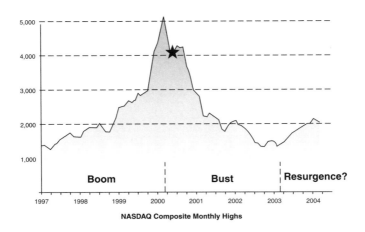

NASDAQ Composite Monthly Highs

Layoffs in the e-tailing industry, unthinkable only a few months ago, have become commonplace. What many people, including employees, thought to be a crown jewel turned out to be made of paste.

6

The shock of a 25 percent drop in the NASDAQ in April, 2000 and the ensuing shyness of venture capitalists to finance dot-coms, the difficulty of obtaining financing via IPOs, and mounting pink slips suggest that the dot-com euphoria is over. It is very unlikely that one can become a sudden billionaire anymore just by moving to Silicon Valley or Austin, Texas, and adding the dot-com moniker to a business.

Layoffs in the e-tailing industry, unthinkable only a few months ago, have become commonplace. Just a few weeks ago all the 230 employees of Emeryville based Reel.com, the largest online DVD and video store, were laid off when the site's IPO was cancelled and the company permanently closed its doors. Investors had poured in over $100 million only a few years earlier thinking it was a sure bet. What many people, including employees, thought to be a crown jewel turned out to be a jewel made of paste.

Recent layoffs have also occurred at companies such as Furniture.com of Framingham, Massachusetts (80 layoffs); Pseudo.com, a streaming video site in New York City (68 layoffs); search engine Alta Vista of Palo Alto (50 layoffs); and APBnews.com, a Wall Street-based crime reporting site (140 layoffs); DrKoop.com, a health care site (50 layoffs); carOrder.com (100 layoffs) and Redwood City-based insurance site, InsWeb (50 lay-offs). Other recent business closures include Verde.com, PetStore.com, and Toysmart. com. In the last few months e-commerce related layoffs total approximately 2,000.

Perhaps the most spectacular dot-com flameout in recent weeks involves the recent liquidation of Boo.com. Until a few months ago this company was the most hip and publi-cized e-commerce company in Europe, selling fashionable and trendy clothes over the Web. The company had a spectacular Web site that included a virtual changing room and 3D graphics, and merchandise prices quoted for 18 countries. The problem was that the company's burn rate was considerably more spectacular than its Web site—$135 million in a two-year period. Boo.com's list of problems reads like a formula for disaster: a poor business plan, followed by poor customer service, poor management, and a Web site that, though visually impressive, was complex and not user-friendly.

The jolt to the e-commerce industry in no way implies the demise of the Internet industry. It is very much alive and doing well. In 1999, Internet-related businesses generated nearly $524 billion in revenues, nearly $200 billion more than in 1998. Internet-related jobs doubled to 2.5 million over 1998 levels. The prospects for the industry as a whole look very good in 2000 and beyond.

What we have been observing in the last six months is a process of separation between those companies that have a sound business proposition and can execute it versus those that do not really have a product or service of value to consumers. This kind of a winnowing of wheat from chaff is a process that we often see in the early stages of most industries. In general it is a healthy process that leads to a stronger industry and better products, and usually, greater customer satisfaction. Too many high-flying dot-coms relied on "mind share" (recognition and a certain degree of loyalty by customers who returned to the company Web site again and again), rather than "market share" (actual sales and their percentage of the total market for that product or service).

There are, of course, winners and losers. Many people are hurt in this process of readjustment. In a recent Bay Area conference, high-tech guru, Mark Andreesen, concluded that as poorly thought out and poorly run dot-coms go out of business, valuable human talent is freed up, and that allows the best new ideas a chance to flourish.

What are some of the lessons from the painful experience of the last few months for emerging dot-coms?

- Hubris is not a substitute for a well-developed business plan.
- Profits are important. One should not tell investors that profits are going to be postponed for a while.
- Watch the money burn rate as well as the people burn rate (I just wonder how long valuable employees can maintain the 24/7 work week, have a life, and maintain productivity?)
- Be flexible and ready to change business plans – adapt to changing markets – one may not get it right the first time. Do not neglect the Old Economy. There are many Internet-related opportunities for reshaping and reinventing older industries such as utilities, auto, travel, insurance, etc.

The e-tailing industry is now trying to make a soft landing. New Economy entrepreneurs must pay greater attention to Old Economy realities such as profits and sound business plans that deal more with value to the customer than stock market valuation.

7

Reality Takes the Wind Out of Online Sales

Perspective: August 2000 ★

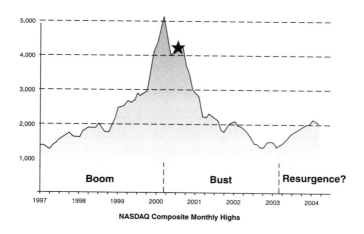

NASDAQ Composite Monthly Highs

In the early stages of the Internet start-up frenzy, it was possible to invest in a company, do an IPO, and cash out before the business model could be proven. Billions of dollars were poured into dot-com companies, even though they possessed the flimsiest of business plans that had little chance of success.

7

Before the memories of the dot-com bomb of last spring begin to fade, and as the NASDAQ begins to climb again, it is time for us to reflect on three questions – what happened? Why did it happen? What are the lessons? Between March 10 and May 23 of this year, the NASDAQ plunged by nearly 37 percent. The market crash was mostly confined to Internet businesses involved in reselling (e-tailing), media, and business-to-business sales. Internet businesses in sectors such as banking, drugs, electronics, finance, flowers, health, media, music, toys, weddings, and beauty are going out of business by the droves.

Internet gurus such as Henry Blodget of Merrill Lynch predict that nearly 75 percent of today's e-commerce companies will go out of business. To put the situation in perspective, we need to remember that the NASDAQ has recovered somewhat from the spring debacle, but the Dow Jones Internet Commerce (DJIC) Index is still down about 50 percent from its March high. But the DJIC index is still up nearly 600 percent since 1998. Despite the spring Internet debacle, the Web has made many people very rich in the past few years.

Over the decades we have had significant market corrections in various industries, including real estate, banking, energy, and computers. What is unique about the recent Internet episode is that we have seldom seen such reckless financing by venture capitalists, investment bankers, and investors of all sizes.

Billions of dollars were poured into companies with the dot-com moniker, even though they possessed the flimsiest of business plans that had little chance of success. This was done in record time with a veneer of due diligence at best. Assessing long-term prospects of a fledgling business meant a time horizon of three months rather than the more typical three to five years.

How could this happen? The answer is fairly straightforward—it was very lucrative for the pros. Billions were made in a matter of a few months. Investment bankers and venture capitalists who launched the IPOs either did not quite understand the intricacies of the Internet economy, were swept away by the euphoria of the "new thing," or saw pure gold in the opportunities. In the early stages of the Internet start-up frenzy, it was possible to invest in a company, do an IPO, and cash out before the business model could be proven. In the rush to make a killing by e-tailing, Old Economy notions such as cash flow and profits seem to have been shelved. It is astounding to discover that of the 39 key companies in the Goldman Sachs Consumer e-Commerce Index there is only one company, eBay, that will show a profit in 2000.

One of our real strengths as a society is our can-do attitude. But in the e-tailing euphoria, this virtue was pushed to its outer limits and became an exercise in futility. Business start-ups were to have materialized in a matter of weeks, with millions of customers hitting the sites to buy the goods in a matter of months.

Many of us as customers were also caught up with the novelty of shopping on the Web. How could we be blamed? The Internet, after all, had done great things for us—e-mail, access to the libraries of the world, e-investing and e-education among others. The reality is that we were all kidding ourselves. The fact is that we love stores. We like to dress up and go there, browse, see and feel the merchandise, kick the tire, exchange pleasantries with the shopkeeper, and say hello to our friends. We are, after all, a nation of shoppers. If e-tailing were to replace going to the store, we would have been doing most of our buying via catalogues a long time ago.

In the United States, catalog purchases amount to 5 percent of all retail sales. This, in a sense, is the realistic limit of the e-tailing market. Even if e-tailing were to capture 50 percent of this market, that would mean 2.5 percent of total retail sales.

The Rise and Fall of Well-Financed E-Tailers

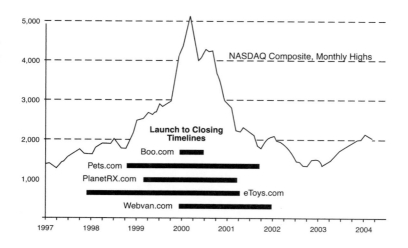

The NASDAQ closing averages between 1998 and 2001 clearly show the incredible rise and meteoric fall in the stock value of many e-tail businesses. Launched in March of 1999, PlanetRx.com's stock rose to $272 - and closed two years later at 27 cents. Some of the most highly publicized (and most highly funded) e-tailers flamed out even faster – Boo.com managed to burn through over $135 million in seven months! Source: NASDAQ

Another major challenge for e-tailing is customer service, particularly with respect to returning merchandise.

The recent trend of growing dot-com alliances with bricks-and-mortar companies makes sense. Many of the e-tailing dot-coms are becoming the online presence for regular businesses. Recent alliances include Lands End and Sears, Amazon.com and Toys R Us, and Rite Aid Drug stores and Drugstore.com. Clicks-and-mortar makes sense to me.

As a real fan of the Internet, I feel better about this development. I would no longer feel guilty about going to the nearest Nordstrom or Wal-Mart and doing some recreational shopping, and then coming back to work and using the Net for communication, information gathering, and word processing.

8

E-Commerce Still Subject to "Old" Economic Principles

Perspective: September 2000 ★

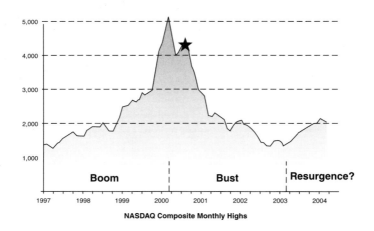

NASDAQ Composite Monthly Highs

Using the Internet to
create new businesses
does not mean that
we throw away sound
economic thinking. The
time has come for us to
think clearly and soundly
and not get caught up in
the current haze of cyber
greed and get rich quick
IPO schemes.

8

Peter Drucker, one of the best known business thinkers of our times, recently said that a startup that calls itself a dot-com will no longer automatically obtain lots of money. The time has come for us to think clearly and soundly rather than get caught up in the current haze of cyber greed and get rich quick IPO schemes.

The Internet is a terrific enabler and provides us with a remarkable worldwide information super-highway. But using it to create new businesses does not mean that we throw away sound economic thinking. Let us consider some of the important principles that need to be considered in starting and sustaining an e-commerce business.

The central problem of e-commerce is product delivery. This is the most expensive and challenging part of the business. What makes sense to me is for the customer to buy on-line and then pick up the merchandise at a nearby distribution center. That means delivery is local. We need to look to the Japanese 7-Eleven chain with nearly 10,000 stores for a successful application of this principle. The customer orders on the Internet and picks up the goods at a neighborhood 7-Eleven. In this case the business does not need to build expensive warehouses or invest in a fleet of trucks.

The chances of success in e-commerce are much greater if the goods traded have a high value-to-weight ratio. Books, CDs, and tapes are such commodities. (It is important to point out that diamonds and gemstones have the highest value-to-weight ratios and thus one of the most desirable e-commerce candidates. However, they don't sell well online because most of us want to see and touch the diamond before we purchase it.)

A book is a perfect e-tailing candidate because the shipping cost is low, it is not fragile, it is not perishable, and it is highly portable. In addition, all over the world, including the U.S., shipping books is highly subsidized. It is the perfect e-tailing product. In light of these economic and physical realities, e-tailing of perishable food articles and low price, high delivery cost commodities will not be a sustainable business proposition.

The importance of converting "mind share" (loyalty to the company's Web site) to "market share" (actual sales) is critical for the success of an e-business. The fact is that "mind share" by itself is an illusion, whereas "market share" is real. The number of hits on a Web site does not mean a thing unless they translate into a sale. What I like about market share is that it means cash flow, and cash flow is king, as far as running a business is concerned. Without cash flow the probability of realizing business profits is zero.

Customer loyalty at any cost does not really make sense unless one is running a charitable organization. In the last year or so millions of dollars have been spent by e-tailing companies to obtain customer "loyalty" by meeting customers' many whims–without worrying about cost or profitability. The case of Kozmo, basically a video delivery service with couriers on bicycle, chronicled in a recent New Yorker article is interesting. In 1999, Kozmo lost $26 million on sales of only $3.6 million. It now plans to layoff several hundred workers, and has postponed its IPO. The company has treated its customers fabulously well. Perhaps too well. Kozmo's courier's process only two orders an hour, and each order amounts to an average of $11. The amazing thing is that every time

Kozmo fills an order the company loses money. Kozmo gets lots of customers, but more customers mean more losses.

The promise of e-commerce was to make it easier and cheaper for businesses to serve customers. Things have not worked out that way for many e-businesses, as they have not used sound economic reasoning in planning their businesses. For viable Internet businesses, such as eBay, and Yahoo, the cost of serving a new customer is miniscule. Delivering content and running auctions for two million customers does not cost any more than serving a million customers. For these companies profits rise as they add more customers. They are indeed the models for the New Economy.

9

Is the New Economy for Real?

Perspective: October 2000 ★

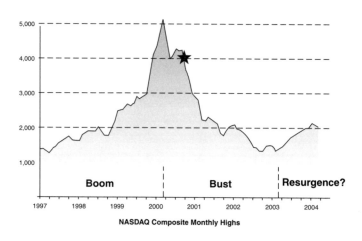

NASDAQ Composite Monthly Highs

There are good reasons for worrying about the robustness of the New Economy in light of recent happenings in financial markets as well as in the economy. Price to earnings ratios do matter, even for Internet stocks.

9

Is the New Economy for real? Is it sustainable? In the past few weeks, I have heard these questions often. There are good reasons for worrying about the robustness of the New Economy in light of recent happenings in financial markets as well as in the economy.

Let us first look at the financial markets:

The Tech Bear Market: Technology stocks have lost more than a quarter of their value since August. The NASDAQ was down to 3,074 on October 12 from its record high of 5,132; it closed Wednesday at 3,171. Internet stocks have fared even worse. The Street.com's Internet Sector Index has fallen 62 percent from its March 2000 peak. The problem is not just with new dot-com start-ups; large-cap top-of-the-line tech stocks are also being battered. As of Wednesday, Amazon.com's stock price had declined by 78 percent from its 52-week high of $113; E*Trade was down to $11.44 from its 52-week high of $40; Yahoo! down to $52.75 from its high of $250; Covad down to $3.56 from its high of $66.

There are several factors underlying the tech stock slide:
- First, slower profit growth resulting from higher energy prices and higher interest rates.
- Second, announcements by major tech firms about lower-than-expected earnings have continued to disappoint investors and analysts. (The average NASDAQ P/E ratio is 115, compared to 21 for the average Dow stock.)

- Third, unfulfilled promises of these high-flying stocks combined with a crisis in the Middle East has precipitated a migration of investors from NASDAQ to Old Economy Dow stocks. Energy, health care, and airline stocks have been particularly attractive as they have gone up by 5 percent to 6 percent since early September in contrast to the 25 percent decline in the tech-heavy NASDAQ stocks.

Let us now look at the economy:

The New Economy is not immune to External Shocks: The New Economy was supposed to have been a near-perfect productivity machine with low inflation thanks to computers, information technology and the Internet. But in the euphoria brought on by inspiring and passionate pronouncements by New Economy icons such as venture capitalist John Doerr, cyber-evangelist Guy Kawasaki and others we forgot about the real world. We perhaps became a tad arrogant and forgot about the power of the oil cartel and the House of Saud. We need to remember that three of the last four U.S. recessions were brought on by a Middle East crisis.

Wealth Effect: Main Street and Wall Street have come closer today than ever. Today, nearly 50 percent of U.S. households own stocks directly or indirectly via pension and mutual funds. Moreover, the stock market is driving the economy more than ever. The wealth effect in light of huge gains in the stock market (often on paper) has been a significant factor in keeping consumer spending in high gear. The significance of this fact becomes obvious when we consider that nearly two-thirds of our economy is dependent on our diligence as consumers in the malls and shopping centers of America. The stock market slide has undoubtedly weakened the impact of the wealth effect on the economy. The decline in net worth of many of our New Economy icons gives us a glimpse of the extent of wealth evaporation in a matter of months – Jeff Bezos, CEO of Amazon.com lost nearly $10 billion in the first nine months of this year; Bill Gates of Microsoft lost $48.5 billion; Paul Allen, also of Microsoft, lost $10 billion in the same period.

Strong Economic Fundamentals: Let us move on to the good news. The current economic expansion is the longest in record. We expect economic growth in 2000 to be at a record 5 percent, unemployment at a near all-time low of 4 percent, and inflation at a modest 3.3 percent. The economy has been on solid ground despite oil price increases and the meltdown of wealth in high places. Since June 1999, the Federal Reserve has increased interest rates six times in order to cool off an overheated economy and engineer a soft landing. The Fed policies are working, and the economy has slowed down considerably in the past several months.

Of course, the soft landing is being hastened considerably by higher oil prices and the problems with equity markets. I do not think that there will be a hard landing, barring an outright Middle East war. The economy will continue to prosper next year at a more sustainable rate as productivity growth continues via economy-wide implementation of information technology and the Internet.

In light of economic and financial market trends summarized above, I have come to the following conclusions:

As far as financial markets are concerned, price-to-earnings ratios do matter, even for Internet or dot-com stocks. You have to demonstrate enormous earnings potential if your P/E ratio is more than 100. This has not happened.

The New Economy businesses are for real, but they have been over-hyped. Peeling off the layers of euphoria, the New

Economy businesses provide us with the infrastructure that has made it possible for us to carry out worldwide commerce as well as information exchange at Internet speed.

Probably the most important lesson from this year's events is that the so-called New Economy still follows the basic principles of economics and finance: a) ultimately, stock prices depend on profits, b) stock prices fall when the product does not deliver the promised value (e.g. tech stocks), c) great wealth can be transitory if it is based on high-risk propositions, d) the business cycle is not dead, and e) the economy is not immune from external shocks.

10

Despite the Web, Location Matters

Perspective: November 2000 ★

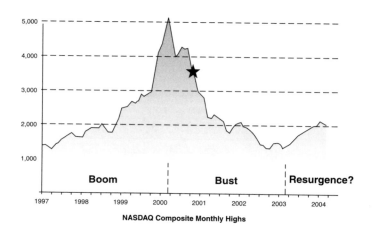

NASDAQ Composite Monthly Highs

The laptop computer, airports, and hotels have become the hub of life in the "placeless" society. Knowledge workers value access to universities, good K-12 education, cultural richness, civic virtue, choice in housing and transportation, diversity of employment opportunities, environmental beauty, good food, and good coffee.

10

The age of the Internet has not only accelerated the speed with which information is gathered and transmitted, it has also redefined our relationship with geography.

Business location decisions, traditionally dependent on Old Economy factors such as access to highways, ports, railroads, and sources of raw material are more and more dependent on our ability to connect with the all important New Economy resources – talent and brain power. Since the 1980s information has increasingly become the key source of wealth, supplanting the primacy of energy and raw materials. As a result, places where human intelligence congregates are the locations that become the centers of prosperity. One could conclude from this that in the digital age the location of a business is no longer determined by the traditional dictates of the Old Economy but more on where people want to live and start their businesses. They do not have to locate their businesses in well-established cities or even prominent high-tech locations such as Silicon Valley or Austin, Texas.

Joel Kotkin, in his recent book, The New Geography, suggests that a feeling of "placelessness" has been surfacing in the last decade since location-related constraints to wealth building no longer appear to be a barrier to business siting. For many New Economy business executives this is a romantic notion made possible by technology. They can work in one country and live in another through telecommunications, frequent flying, and frequent use of hotels – a highly nomadic, exhausting, and unsustainable lifestyle. The laptop computer, airports, and hotels have become the hub of life in the "placeless" society. Extending this "placelessness" notion further some futurists, including William Mitchell, argue that the cities of the future are essentially anti-spatial. In other words, the world wide computer network has become the world wide market place, and it is redefining not only our businesses but also our communities and urban life.

I disagree with the "placelessness" theorists. I think that in the digital age location matters a great deal. It matters because knowledge workers are a fairly sophisticated bunch. They value access to universities as well as good K-12 education, cultural richness, civic virtue, choice in housing and transportation, diversity of employment opportunities, environmental beauty, good food, and good coffee (the beverage of choice in the New Economy).

In light of this it is not surprising that *Fortune* magazine (November 27, 2000) ranks the following as the best cities for business: 1) New York City, 2) San Francisco, 3) Chicago, 4) Washington, D.C. area, and 5) San Jose. Except for San Jose (a.k.a. capital of Silicon Valley), all of these cities are old American business capitals that stand out because they have not only met the challenges of the New Economy but also made technology their source of growth. They have truly reinvented their future. The criteria for selecting these cities included a) business environment, b) cost of doing business, c) quality of local workforce, and d) quality of life.

San Francisco's ranking may be surprising to many in the Bay Area in light of its old image of "Baghdad by the Bay" – a beautiful city with a penchant for regulation. But here are some startling facts about San Francisco in the context of the New Economy: it is the world capital for digital media and a major hub for e-commerce, software, and content development. This is the result of a unique melding of techies from Silicon Valley with the highly creative, entrepreneurial, and financial expertise that is drawn to this city.

- More than 1,000 technology firms employ 40,000 people
- San Francisco has enormous strength in New Economy business services—web designers, intellectual property attorneys, and computer services people
- The city is well wired for heavy Internet traffic
- Once a depressed area, the south of Market Street area in the city has experienced a New Economy renaissance in the last seven years that is most impressive
- San Francisco is the cultural capital of the Bay Area and a safety valve for thousands of young knowledge workers trying to escape the cultural vacuum of Silicon Valley
- It is a compact city that is vibrant, exciting, and attractive—a magnet for knowledge workers despite the high real estate prices

There are other, older cities that did not appear in the *Fortune* magazine list that possess attributes similar to San Francisco and have reinvented their future in the context of the New Economy. These include Seattle, Boston, and Denver. By contrast, many of the former icons of Industrial America such as St. Louis, Detroit, and Newark have never been able to a make a real transition to the New Economy and thus they have not regained their glory days.

Benefits of places like San Francisco have been enormous for peripheral communities of the Bay Area including Silicon Valley, the rapidly growing tech-savvy East Bay, and Marin County. The New Economy communities prosper from good

lifestyles as well as a good quality of life. A culturally- and aes-
thetically-rich city like San Francisco becomes a catalyst and
agent of economic vitality for the entire region. This can be
easily observed by the arts, entertainment, upscale shopping,
and restaurant linkages between San Francisco and peripheral cities such as Walnut Creek, Mill Valley, and Palo Alto.
Of course the peripheral cities have the added advantage of
greater open space, more recreational opportunities, and usually greater choice in housing.

Places such as San Francisco and Seattle are critical to the
success of the digital economy as they also provide another
ingredient knowledge workers want – a place to meet for creative people who need to interact face to face on an informal
basis while enjoying their surroundings. These places provide
them with a sense of community as well as networking – in-
gredients critical for success not only in the New Economy
but also in the next economy.

11

The Internet is
No Panacea for Business

Perspective: February 2001 ★

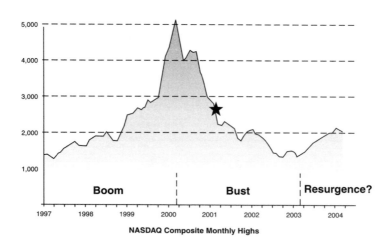

NASDAQ Composite Monthly Highs

The dot-com meltdown has changed the e-commerce landscape. We have moved from irrational exuberance to irrational pessimism. Both views are harmful for our businesses as well as the economy.

11

Although the Internet has been an enormous success for all of us, the marriage of the Internet and business has been painful at best. Only a year ago the formation of a new dot-com meant investors rushing to fund the venture without even checking out the viability of the business plan. Funding for businesses with little or no prospects of revenues (and thus no profits) was not uncommon. It meant using up millions of dollars in a matter of days in expensive commercials for a service that really was untested. For many bright young people (with no business experience) it conjured up images of instant wealth. For many New Economy entrepreneurs it meant replacing traditional stores with online retailers. All you had to do was to establish a Web presence and start making money – it was a gold rush to the Web. The dot-com market meltdown and thousands of dot-com layoffs in the past three months have changed the e-commerce landscape. We have moved from a period of irrational exuberance, where a dot-com could do no wrong, to irrational pessimism, where the Web is seen as a barren habitat for business. Both of these views are unrealistic and harmful for our businesses as well as the economy.

First, e-commerce is not dead. There are companies that are successful and have a good chance of staying around for a long time in one incarnation or other. The list includes eBay, Amazon.com, AOL Time Warner, Travelocity.com, Expedia Inc., Homestore.com and a few others. Second, the collapse of the dot-coms should not lull bricks and mortar businesses into complacency. It is a great opportunity for them to hire talented ex-dot-com employees (Web dudes without their Porsches) and to continue to digitize their traditional businesses.

I think that it is critical for the success of current and future e-commerce business to keep in mind the lessons learned from the dot-com debacle. There are four key lessons:

- Need for a robust business plan: A Web-based business is a business, and it must have a realistic business plan with a clear path to profitability. Pouring millions of dollars into commercials, or the speed of the Internet alone, will not rescue a poorly thought-out business.

- It is people and not technology: A Web-based business is not just about technology; it is about customers and suppliers. It is not possible to run a successful e-business if customers and suppliers do not want to buy or sell via the Internet because of habit and strong relationships or legal intricacies.

- Growing a business the old fashioned way: Businesses take time to grow and Web-based businesses are no exception to this rule. Many venture capitalists did not provide a second round of funding for viable dotcoms because of expectations that the firm should have become profitable overnight.

- Clicks do not mean money: A hit on a Web site does not automatically convert into revenue. This has been a difficult lesson to absorb for a large number of cyberentrepreneurs. Spending millions on advertising and Web-glitz may attract a lot of virtual window shoppers, but that does not mean they will buy from the site. The business has to provide real value to the site visitors before they will take out their charge card.

Digitizing a conventional bricks-and-mortar business does not just mean selling on the Internet. It means the use of digital technologies to solve key business problems as well as expanding business options. The goal is not just to embrace technology but enhance business possibilities. Slywotzky and Morrison in a recent edition of the Harvard Management Update discuss key areas of business improvement via digitization. These include:

- Knowing what the customer wants: A business via an interactive online relationship can determine which products a customer wants before the production and distribution wheels are set in motion. The result is higher efficiency and customer satisfaction.

Sky-High P/E Ratios: Recipe for Disaster

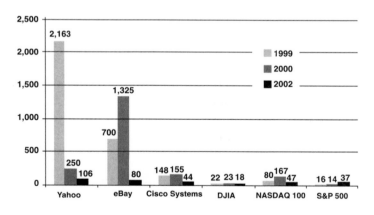

Historically, the S&P 500 average stock price-to-earnings (P/E) ratio has hovered around 16. During the peak of the dot-com euphoria, P/E ratios for Yahoo!, eBay and other Internet companies skyrocketed – at least for a while. P/E ratios do matter even for Internet or dot-com stocks. Stock prices depend on profits. Prices fall when the product does not deliver the promised value (e.g. tech stocks). Sources: Yahoo! Finance, Charles Schwab

- Instant communication of information: By linking various departments of a business via the Internet, company management can obtain vital data in real time instead of waiting for the traditional quarterly report.
- Rapid customer service: Increasingly, customers prefer making an online request for customer service. The example of Cisco Systems is striking—today 85 percent of customer support requests are online compared to only 10 percent in 1994.
- Enhancing employee productivity: All businesses can gain enormously by shifting workers to higher value added activities by digitizing repetitive and boring tasks. Productivity can also be increased via in-house online training of employees.

The Internet has changed our lives in very real terms, and it is changing our businesses profoundly. But access to a new technology does not mean that making money is any easier today than it was in the past. I am afraid that it has to be done in an old fashioned way—by conceiving and running sound businesses. Now that the gee-whiz era of e-commerce is over, we need to fix it and move forward to a more realistic and sustainable base.

12

Tulips, Manias
and Bubbles

Perspective: May 2001 ★

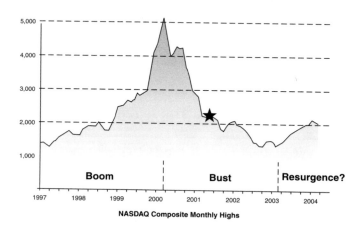

NASDAQ Composite Monthly Highs

The economy is subject to recurrent episodes of speculative fever and manias with accompanying financial euphoria followed by financial ruin for many. But despite the collapse of the dot-com bubble the Internet will continue to enrich our lives as well as enhance our businesses and our economies.

12

The highly productive market economy has bestowed enormous economic benefits for nearly a century. But one thing we forget is that the economy is subject to recurrent episodes of speculative fever and manias, with accompanying financial euphoria followed by financial ruin for many.

The most notable speculative episodes in the last three centuries include the 17th century Tulip Mania in Western Europe, the 18th century South Sea Company bubble, the crash of 1929, and the junk bond fiasco of the 1980s. To this list I would have to add the Internet Bubble (and dot-com debacle) of 2000-01.

First, I will sketch the key elements of the first and last of these speculative episodes and then look at the common thread running through them and see what we can learn from history. One hopes, of course, that we can avoid getting caught up in such bubbles and prevent departures from reason, but that may be asking too much.

The first world-class financial bubble occurred in the 1630s in Holland. It did not involve stocks or bonds, but tulip bulbs. The episode was so spectacular that it got its own name—Tulip Mania. The tulip, with nearly 160 species, first came to Western Europe in the 16th century from Constantinople. The tulip, beautiful and varied in color, was greatly appreciated in Europe and its cultivation and display endowed great prestige to the nobles who possessed them. Tulips became an obsession of the well-to-do. Supply/demand forces went into action and the market responded with prices of bulbs skyrocketing. Some rare bulbs were selling for as much as $50,000, and by 1636, stores selling bulbs were established in the Amsterdam stock market. According to Charles MacKay in *Extraordinary Popular Delusions and the Madness of Crowds*, the tulip dealers speculated on the bulbs and became rich by purchasing when prices fell and selling when the prices increased.

The conventional wisdom at that time was that the tulip madness was going to last forever. Everyone joined in to get a piece of the action – from noblemen to farmers and from sailors to chimney sweeps. People sold their homes and real property to buy tulip bulbs. People borrowed money with their possessions as collateral in an effort to leverage their tulip buying power. Tulip Mania went global and enormous amounts of money poured into Holland from all corners of the world. By 1637 the tulip bubble had come to an end. A selling frenzy took over, prices plummeted and many lost all they had, with some declaring bankruptcy. The precipitous fall of tulip prices and enormous loss of wealth resulted in a severe economic downturn in Holland.

There was one saving grace. The tulip survived and flourished. An international market for flowers and bulbs has developed over the last two centuries with stable and reasonable prices. The tulip, to this day, remains a symbol of Holland and is enjoyed all over the world.

The Internet is a path-breaking technological advance that continues to change the way we live and the way we do business. By 1999 Silicon Valley pundit John Doerr claimed that the Internet boom would be larger than the personal computer (PC) boom. This was confirmed later that year – the market wealth created by the Internet stood at $235 billion versus $221 billion by the PC. This spectacular growth did not go unnoticed by individual investors as well as the venture capital (VC) industry. In 1998 the venture capital industry invested nearly $17 billion in Internet-related startups – an all time record. A virtual tidal wave of capital moved into Internet-related companies between 1998 and 1999. Companies like Healtheon and eBay saw their stock prices go up by 3,000 percent. This was a situation where very high share prices were sustained by the unbridled enthusiasm of investors. In addition, enormous media hype via 24-hour TV coverage of economic matters, as if they were sporting events, continued to promise miracles that were certainly not apparent using sound analysis. In light of the Internet euphoria it is not surprising that a significant body of financial analysts were perfectly comfortable with price-to-earnings ratios of 300.

Venture capital firms were not at all reluctant to finance companies that, at best, had half-baked business plans with no obvious chance of generating revenue. It was enough to have a few thousand hits (and no cash flow) on a Web site to justify impressive share valuations in the go-go years of the Internet.

Often the outlandish valuations were justified in the name of the New Economy. (The New Economy is about speed, communication, and networks and not about "bad economics.") It is amazing that in many cases companies floating their initial public offerings had no prior record of profit. It must be noted that the e-commerce icon Amazon. com has yet to show a profit after several years of operation.

Money-losing dot-coms had market valuations that became the envy of the most successful corporations in the United States. There were, of course, big winners. Young entrepreneurs of companies such as Yahoo!, eBay, Amazon. com and owners of VC firms and investment bankers made billions in a matter of months. In the surreal dot-com world fortunes were made and lost in a matter of days.

The dot-com bubble burst by mid-2000. The tech-heavy NASDAQ dropped by more than 50 percent in a matter of months, wiping out nearly $1.5 trillion of wealth. Today the list of expired dot-coms reads like the Who's Who of the Internet world and tens of thousands of dot-comers are unemployed. And small-time investors are left to foot the bill as their retirement savings and children's education funds have disappeared into thin air.

Despite the collapse of the dot-com bubble the Internet is here to stay and it will continue to enrich our lives as well as enhance our businesses and our economies just as the tulip did not disappear after the Tulip Mania.

What are the common themes underlying speculative bubbles such as the dot-com frenzy, Tulip Mania, the crash of 1929, etc.?

- Euphoria and escape from reality into fantasy land
- A short memory for financial disasters (or lack of knowledge about them)
- Promotion of untested and unrealistic ideas as brilliant discoveries by a youthful and enormously self-confident group of people
- Unrealistic expectation about new technologies and their potential as huge moneymakers. (For example, it has been extremely difficult to make money with a pure Internet play business.)
- Erroneous relationship between large sums of money flowing into an area and high probability of success. (Billions of dollars went into the dot-coms in the 1998-99 period.)

12 - Tulips, Manias and Bubbles

Despite enormous economic and social costs inflicted in the aftermath of a speculative disaster such as the Tulip Mania of the 17th century or the very recent dot-com debacle, I doubt very much that we will avoid future bubbles. This is due to our desire to make a fast buck, the excitement of the ride, and the opportunities in a free market economy to take risks. Is there anything we can do? I do not suggest more regulation of the economy (that would make the economy less efficient) or regulation of mass hysteria (that would make it a more oppressive society). The only viable and realistic thing to do is to become thoughtful and careful when a particular invention or discovery promises the moon. In other words, practice due diligence as well as you can.

13

Making E-tailing Work

Perspective: July 2001 ★

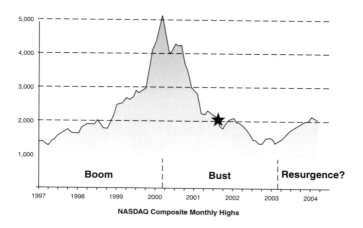

NASDAQ Composite Monthly Highs

The failure of the premier online grocer Webvan is likely to be a classic case study for business schools for years to come. Webvan did not understand the sociology and psychology of shopping for food in America.

13

Concerns about the future of "e-tailing" grows with the recent Chapter 7 bankruptcy filing by cyber-grocer giant Webvan.com. Concurrent with the bankruptcy filing, the company laid off 2,000 employees. The demise of Webvan has dealt a severe financial blow to investors. The "money burn" between its initial funding in 1996 and now has been close to a billion dollars. The venture capital (VC) firms impacted include VC icons such as Benchmark Capital, Sequoia Capital, Softbank Corp., the Barksdale Group, Yahoo! Inc, and E*Trade Group Inc.

The failure of the premier online grocer Webvan is likely to be a classic case study for business schools for years to come. Why did Webvan fail? There are many reasons:

Incorrect Business Model – the company appears to have assumed that they were in a technology business and not in a grocery supermarket business.

Lack of Appropriate Talent – Webvan was a Web-based supermarket run by people with no apparent retail experience. This is a business with very thin margins where the best of the food management world can lose its shirt. Consultants, techies, and others with no apparent food experience were made officers and directors. The CEO George Shaheen, former chief of a major consulting firm, Arthur Anderson Inc., had little or no food related experience. The founder of Webvan, Louis Borders (also the founder of Borders Books) was an expert in selling books, but books do not expire or go rancid.

Lack of Understanding of the Sociology of Food Retailing—The management refused to acknowledge how consumers shop for food. People like to be in a supermarket looking at the merchandise, seeing it, even feeling it (hopefully only occasionally). Buying food is a tactile as well as a social experience. Most people like to speak to the grocer, the butcher, the wine department manager, and so on. For people not to go to the market there has to be special reason. Webvan did not understand the sociology and psychology of shopping for food in America.

Lack of Demographic Understanding—Webvan located major warehouses in Atlanta and Los Angeles and in both locations people are used to driving and would rather drive to the store than wait for a delivery. Only transplants from congested metro areas with both spouses working would warm up to the Webvan idea. Webvan's problems became very serious in Orange County and San Diego County, both of which have large Latin American and Asian populations, and where local merchants meet the diverse needs of the various ethnic communities much more effectively than Webvan possibly could.

Erroneous Target Marketing—The most obvious target customers for the company were not the upscale suburban families or stay-at-home moms but the people who had problems getting to the grocery store. The obvious customers were in senior centers, college fraternities, mothers with very young children, the disabled, late night workers, and, of course, the upscale "dot-com" people.

High Cost of Running an Online Grocery Business— The cost of building Webvan's high-tech Atlanta warehouse alone was a staggering $40 million —a whole lot more than a traditional grocery warehouse for retail chains. Webvan used the latest technology to automate its warehouses, they had to buy a fleet of hundreds of refrigerated delivery trucks, and pay for insured drivers all over the country. By offering home delivery, online grocers had to bear the cost of the "last mile" in the transaction, a cost that traditional grocery stores don't have.

The demise of Webvan does not mean that the online retail industry is not viable. According to the trade group Shop.org, by the end of 2000, 72 percent of catalog retailers, 43 percent of store-centered retailers, and 27 percent of on-line retailers were running sound (profitable) businesses. The key to their success is that they understand that the Internet is another tool in a portfolio of communication options. The successful companies also understand the importance of target marketing and market segmentation. Here is a list of success stories:

WalMart.com – The company has benefited significantly by redesigning its Web site to focus on those things that customers like buying online rather than trying to sell everything they carry in their stores.

Amazon.com – The company consistently attracts large amounts of online traffic (recent count 22 million users) via key partnerships and sells items that range from CD's, toys, tools, and electronics to prescription drugs. The company is the largest online bookseller. Amazon.com is likely to become profitable by the fourth quarter of 2001. (Let us hope so!)

1-800-Flowers.com – This company sells fresh flowers and gifts via its toll-free numbers as well as the Internet. The key to their success is good communication with customers, including live chat sessions and e-mails with customers.

Sephora.com – This online cosmetic company did what the dot-com world initially thought was blasphemy. Realizing that the Internet was not sufficient they created store-fronts – a good example of the "clicks-and-bricks" approach.

The next generation of New Economy grocery stores include the Safeways and Albertsons of the world. In the last few days of the demise of Webvan, the nationwide grocery chain Albertsons has seen a sudden surge of online orders via their Web site (Albertsons.com). This Old Economy company uses its stores as distribution hubs. They also plan to take online orders for pick-up by customers—no expensive trucks, drivers with starched uniforms, or $40 million warehouses.

Safeway is partnering with Tesco, a UK-based multinational grocery chain with successful Internet experience, to use the Internet in a smart way and not repeat Webvan's mistakes.

E-tailing works, but not the Webvan way. The Old Economy grocers such as Safeway and Albertsons are using the Internet the smart way and proving that far from being di-nosaurs they are the wave of the future.

Webvan: From IPO to Bankruptcy

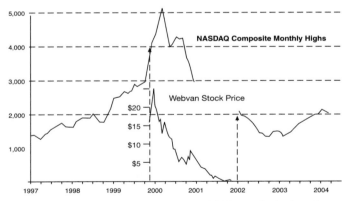

Webvan, with a successful IPO in November 1999, saw its stock go from a peak of $25 then fall almost steadily to its bankruptcy in December 2001. Webvan's decline foreshadowed (and contributed to) the crash in Internet stocks that followed soon after. Source: NASDAQ

14

Don't Judge the Net
on Financial Success
Alone

Perspective: February 2002 ★

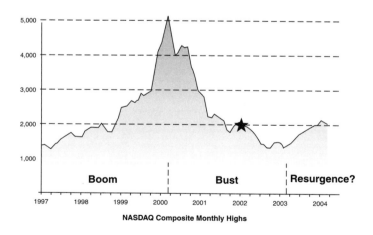

NASDAQ Composite Monthly Highs

Today, e-learning is opening new doors for the fastest-growing component of higher education. Peter Drucker suggested that the cultural impact of the Internet may be more significant than the economic impact.

14

One of the problems assessing new technologies is that the common yardstick used is financial success in the marketplace. The question heard most often relating to the success of a new technology is—can it make money? This is all well and good in our highly successful market economy where financing of research and development is frequently tied to the prospect of commercial success. But success relating to the debut of a new technology must be measured in much broader terms which include quality-of-life considerations such as improvements in our health, the environment, and learning.

I have a concern in that the aftermath of the dot-com bomb and the "telecom fizzle out" we may undervalue the Internet because it has been a challenge making money with it. My concern is heightened by our temptation of equating value (and performance) with the size and profitability of an industry. The Internet, without question, is of great importance to mankind, but on its own may not be a large industry.

Movies probably have had a greater impact on human imagination than the Internet, but on a global (or a national) scale they have not amounted to a large industry. If the movie industry were to cease to exist today, the economic impact would be felt mostly in Hollywood and Bollywood (India).

The Internet has not amounted to a large industry so far, but it has had enormous impact on us. The single biggest impact of the Internet is the conquest of distance well beyond the telephone and the fax from a communications point of view. In addition to its economic impact, the Internet also has a very significant cultural impact worldwide. Peter Drucker in a recent interview (*Business 2.0*, October 2001) suggested that the cultural impact may be more significant than the economic impact. Case in point is the way the Internet has enabled many U.S. companies to transfer their call centers to distant places like Bangalore, India, which has a large, well-educated, English-speaking population. The call center employees go to special schools to speak English with an American accent in order to increase the comfort level of U.S. customers. The important thing here is that many of these workers do not see themselves just as citizens of a developing economy but increasingly as part of the global middle class.

From my perspective, the most significant breakthrough that the Internet has created is in the area of e-learning. The Internet is thriving in the halls of academia. More than 50 percent of 4,000 U.S. colleges and universities in this country now provide courses online. According to the U.S. Distance Learning Association, nearly 2 million students take online courses annually, and that is likely to expand to more than 5 million by 2006. Today, e-learning is opening new doors for the fastest-growing component of higher education – working adults. The need for online learning can only increase in the coming years.

Examples of major e-learning institutions range from the University of Maryland (www.umuc.edu), which offers online courses and 70 degrees and certificates to its 63,000 students, to the U.S. Army's Virtual University (www.eArmyU.com) founded by a coalition of 19 western states in 1997.

So far, e-learning success has come to established universities with good brand names that have been able to reach out to working adults. Among for-profit e-learning colleges, there is only one star—the University of Phoenix.

In addition to a brand name, there is the challenge of quality. There are concerns in many colleges and universities about faculty time allocation between e-learning and on-campus students. Many elite universities such as Harvard and MIT are concerned about diluting the value of their brand name by providing online degrees.

Although the MIT faculty voted not to support online teaching, it embarked on an amazing strategy to support online education. MIT now plans to bring the lecture notes and assignments for most of its courses online free of charge. There are no online degrees from MIT, but there is access to the knowledge of its world-class faculty. I think that it is a great idea.

Many education experts argue that no online learning experience can replace the value of a real-life campus educational experience. I agree with that conclusion. But the growing needs of the working population and business training needs are a most appropriate niche for Web-based learning. For a knowledge-based economy, the Internet is essential.

15

The New Economy
Gets a Bad Name

Perspective: April 2002 ★

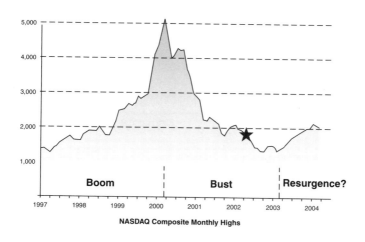

NASDAQ Composite Monthly Highs

In the minds of many, the term "New Economy" is associated with huge stock market losses or the loss of thousands of tech jobs. Instead of brooding about the failed promise of the New Economy, we should focus on how the Internet has shaped our lives and businesses and where it is likely to lead us in the future.

15

With the dot-com bomb of 2000-01, there is considerable skepticism about the validity of the concept of the "New Economy." As a matter of fact, today most of my professional colleagues avoid using the term altogether.

The reasons for this loss of credibility are, to a considerable extent, psychological. In the minds of many, the term "New Economy" is associated with huge stock market losses (fall of the NASDAQ from 5,000 to 1,600) running into a trillion dollars or more. For others, it is associated with the loss of thousands of "tech" jobs and a major jolt to the careers of many freshly minted MBAs.

But there are other reasons for the term's bad name—bad analysis and hype. Many analysts, the media, and even venture capitalists appear to have used the rubric of the "New Economy" to justify such wildly preposterous things as:

- The viability of running a business successfully without a business plan—the same approach as kids running a lemonade stand on a summer afternoon
- Profits are not important for a business as long as it captures the minds of those clicking on the Web site
- Lending money to a start-up without conducting due diligence
- A NASDAQ market capitalization of 245 times earnings (considered sustainable in March 2000)
- The death of the business cycle, resulting in a world of unending prosperity without interruption (the econ-

omy had become so resilient that it could overcome external shocks such as wars, natural disasters, and large-scale terrorism)

- A little digging into history reveals that "speculative bubbles" usually are accompanied by hypes of a "new era" of prosperity. Herbert Hoover (the 31st president of the United States) pronounced that the end of poverty was within our grasp in 1928. (The Great Depression started in 1929). By citing the famous forecast of President Hoover, I am not suggesting that we are in any way on the verge of an economic disaster. I am just pointing out that large speculative events like the very recent dot-com debacle usually have a common formula: unmitigated greed, unrealistic expectations, poor analysis and hype.

The fundamental fact underlying the demise of the dot-coms is the mistaken premise that a new technology (the Internet) is inherently a moneymaker and has a built-in business model. The fact is that it is a tool with which a business can create a useful product or service that people value and are willing to pay for. Having a new technology does not give us the license to mint money.

It is important to recognize and assess the contributions that the Internet has made to our way of doing business, learning, and communicating. To do this objectively, it is important that we not use the term New Economy when we refer to all things associated with the Internet and its uses. I would even go so far as to say that we stop using the term New Economy altogether in an analytical context. Why? Because the rules of mainstream economics are all valid when we analyze and discuss Internet-related businesses and their impact on the economy.

Instead of brooding about the failed promise of the New Economy, we should focus on the ways the Internet has shaped our lives and businesses in the past several years and where it is likely to lead us in the future.

The Internet provides an inexpensive, fast, and flexible means of communications for millions of people around the globe. The use of e-mail in our households and businesses is commonplace. Law enforcement uses the Internet to track down criminals. Our churches, community groups, and clubs use it to stay in touch with their membership. The Internet is used for research, banking, checking weather, buying airline tickets, making hotel reservations, and listening to

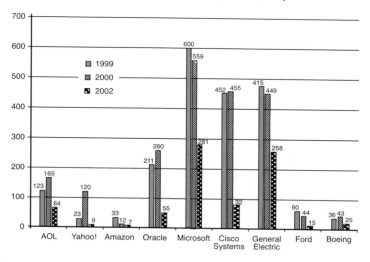

New Economy Trumps Old Economy
Market Capitalizations (in $ billions)

Microsoft's market capitalization is larger than that of Ford, General Electric and Boeing combined. This would have been unthinkable only a few years ago.
Sources: Yahoo! Finance, Charles Schwab

music, among other things. These are good things, and for a large number of us it makes our lives easier and perhaps more enjoyable. But the fundamental question is: will the Internet boost productivity (key to our standard of living) substantially throughout the economy over the long haul?

Economists Robert Litan and Alice Rivlin (*Beyond the Dot-coms*, Brookings Institution, 2001) estimate that the Internet could boost our annual productivity by 0.4 percent a year. This is a substantial number, and it will make a difference. In arriving at this number, the authors assumed that the Net would generate healthy productivity gains in financial services, health care, and government services. The concern I have is that productivity gains in these sectors have been lagging for quite some time despite the Internet. I hope they are right, and the Internet lives up to some of its early promise.

There is little doubt that the Internet does not change everything as proclaimed by the New Economy enthusiasts of the late 1990s. It does, however, change some things—mostly in communications.

How does the Internet stack up in comparison with great inventions of history? Robert Gordon, a well-known economist at Northwestern University, has compared the Internet with plumbing, the automobile, radio, and television. His conclusion—the aforementioned inventions have had greater impact on our lives than the Internet.

Robert Gordon may or may not be right, and only time will tell. Ultimately, the Internet will be judged by its impact on health, longevity, and our personal and business efficiency. The promise of the Internet is very much present, despite the set-back of the dot-com bomb.

16

Silicon Valley After the Dot-com Bomb

Perspective: July 2002 ★

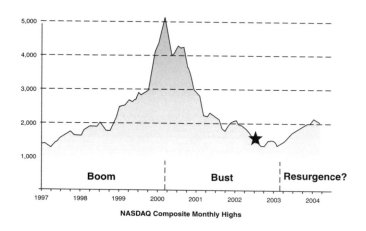

NASDAQ Composite Monthly Highs

Silicon Valley's primacy in high technology is a result of the extraordinary convergence of science, technology, innovation, entrepreneurship, and venture capital. The most promising emerging area of innovation involves the convergence of biotechnology and information technology in areas such as bioinformatics, biomaterials, and biochips.

16

For several decades the Bay Area in general and Silicon Valley in particular have been one of the most dynamic and prosperous economic regions in the world. The region's primacy in high technology is a result of the extraordinary convergence of science, technology, innovation, entrepreneurship, and venture capital. But now, with the recession of 2001 and the dot-com bomb of 2002, what is the future direction of the Silicon Valley economy?

First, here is a brief history of waves of innovations in Silicon Valley:

Aerospace and Defense (1950s and 1960s) – The region's defense and aerospace industries received a great deal of stimulus from the Korean War, the Cold War, and the space race with the Russians. The region's electronics infrastructure was built in this period and it paved the way for the next wave of innovation. The era came to an end with defense cutbacks between 1969-71. (The aerospace industry received a further setback with end of the Cold War in the early 1990s.)

Semiconductors and Integrated Circuits (1960s and 1970s) – The invention of integrated circuits using semiconductors in 1959 spawned nearly 30 semiconductor firms in the Valley, including Fairchild, Intel, AMD, and National Semiconductor. Nearly 90 percent of the semiconductor firms in the United States were in the Silicon Valley in the period 1959-76. The microprocessor was developed at Intel in this period; this led to the development of the personal computer.

Personal Computer (1970s and 1980s) – The development of the microprocessor and special chips paved the way for the personal computer. This was a period of explosive growth for the region in jobs and wealth, as Silicon Valley became the high-tech capital of the world. In 1975, there were only 830 firms (100,000 jobs) in the Valley and by 1990 the number of firms had risen to 3,000 (267,000 jobs). The development and widespread use of PC's led to the next stage of innovation – the Internet.

Internet (1990s) – With the Gulf War-induced recession and the end of the Cold War, the Valley entered a period of anemic growth as business people looked for the next area of opportunity. The answer was the commercial development of the Internet. Soon the region became the world leader in Internet businesses, with the emergence of firms including Cisco Systems, Yahoo! and Netscape, among others. In 1992-98, software jobs in the valley increased by 150 percent. Software, computer, and networking firms reaped an unprecedented bonanza from the dot-com "boom."

The dot-com bubble started to inflate as billions of venture capital dollars and IPO money poured into Internet-related businesses that were hastily put together with little business planning but a great deal of hubris. The rest is history as the tech-heavy NASDAQ crashed in March 2000 after technology stocks were driven to ridiculous levels. Ever since March 2000 we have been in the "bust" phase of the boom-bust cycle. (Historically these cycles have been associated with the commercialization of major new technologies such as railroads, electricity, telephone, and radio.) Despite the bust, the Internet is alive and well and brings us great value. But it has been difficult to make money with it.

The trillion-dollar question is what innovation is likely to drive the next phase of Silicon Valley's development?

The most promising emerging area of innovation (and economic development) involves the convergence of biotechnology and information technology in areas such as bioinformatics, biomaterials, and biochips:

Bioinformatics: The commercial application of genomics depends to a large extent on information technologies that help in discovering and developing new products. The enormous amount of data generated by developments in genomics requires enormous amounts of data processing to develop new medicines and cures for illnesses.

The Bay Area has major competitive advantage in this emerging field due to the existence of firms such as Applied Biosystems, Celera Genomics, and Nanogen. In addition, IBM and Sun Microsystems have joined a consortium of 40 life sciences organizations and formed the "I3C" organization with the goal of speeding up genomics and protein research. Finally, the software giant Oracle has launched a major collaborative venture with Hitachi and Myriad Genetics to carry out further research-and-development activity in this vital area.

Biochips: The need for making things smaller and smaller in information technology products is never ending, and biochips is the technology for the next generation of integrated circuits that work at the molecular level. Examples of the success in this area include the partnership between Genecor (Palo Alto) and Dow Chemical that is involved in producing optical switches. The leading U.S. biochip company, Santa Clara based Affymetrix, has been involved in a major breakthrough that deposits bits of DNA, rather than transistors, on computer chips.

Biomaterials: New materials for agriculture, manufacturing (such as Dupont's bacteria-based "3GT" fibers), and time-released seeds produced by Landec are excellent examples of this new field. Silicon Valley and the East Bay region (Alameda, Contra Costa and Solano counties) are well positioned to become world leaders in the next generation of these "convergence industries" in light of their enormous strength in information technology as well as biosciences.

But despite the great promise of the Bay Area in the Next Economy of "convergent technologies" we have to be vigilant. We must not repeat the terrible mistakes of the dot-com bust where we had all the advantages in the world, including great technology, talent, and money, and we still blew it. Technology commercialization is not a slam-dunk under the best of conditions. We must not repeat the mistakes of the dot-com era but move ahead with the lessons learned with a great deal of enthusiasm. The Bay Area cannot afford to miss this opportunity.

17

If You Build It,
They May Not Come

Perspective: July 2002 ★

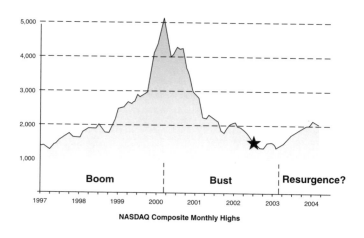

NASDAQ Composite Monthly Highs

The fatal assumption of the telecom industry was "build and they will come." This is always a highly dangerous assumption. Supply does not always create its own demand.

17

In the past two years, we have paid a great deal of attention to the dot-com debacle. But it is absolutely shocking to realize now that the impact of the telecomunications industry meltdown is several magnitudes larger. The decline in the equity markets, loss of employment, erosion of retirement nest eggs, and loss of confidence in our business leaders due to fraudulent accounting and other unethical transgressions.

The crash of the nation's second-largest long-distance company, WorldCom (parent of MCI), underscores the seriousness of the problem. The WorldCom bankruptcy, larger than the Enron case, is the biggest bankruptcy ever in the United States. The impact of the WorldCom crash has serious consequences for its shareholders, employees, and customers. Another impact of the WorldCom debacle is on state pension funds that hold WorldCom bonds. The states with largest exposures include California ($507 million), Washington ($247 million), Texas ($220 million), New York ($194 million), and Massachusetts ($178 million).[1]

The problems of the telecom industry are not just limited to WorldCom. Two other large players, Global Crossing and Qwest Communications, are currently being investigated for accounting irregularities.

Workers are also feeling the impact of the telecom crisis. A recent estimate by Challenger, Gray & Christmas, a human resources database firm, suggests that more than half a million telecom workers, such as operators and supply-chain employees, have been laid off since the beginning of 2001.

What are the reasons underlying the telecom crash? The first and foremost is excess capacity in the industry (building of more telecom networks than the market warranted). This trend originated in the heady days of the Internet-triggered dot-com era (1997–1999) when no assumption about a business model seemed to be outlandish. The fatal assumption was "build and they will come." This is always a highly dangerous assumption. Supply does not always create its own demand. It certainly did not happen with telecoms.

The problem has been that telecom demand for Internet use in the past four years (1997–2001) has only doubled every year, but the telecom industry added on to its fiberoptic network at an unbelievable rate that assumed demand doubled every 100 days. This meant an increase in network capacity of nearly 500 times, while demand increased only four times.[2] Too many firms building the same networks in the United States as well as in Europe further exacerbated the problem of excess capacity.

The bottom line for the industry has been that billions of dollars have been spent on building capacity for which there is no demand. The transportation analogy would be building millions of miles of freeways with no cars to use them. The building frenzy has resulted in a trillion-dollar debt for the industry, which is becoming a serious challenge for the industry to service.

The other problem for the industry has been the accounting scandals and loss of credibility in management, as executives feathered their nests exercising their stock options at highly inflated prices. During Global Crossing's heyday, CEO Gary Winnick's stock sale take amounted to an astounding $750 million. Previous Chief Operating Officer David Lee's take was $216 million, and Senior Vice

President Barry Porter's take was $174 million.[3] The result of this pattern of executive compensation has been massive erosion of public confidence in the telecom sector.

What does it all mean for a critical infrastructure industry that basically defines our 21st century lifestyle as well as commerce?

- Other bankruptcies in the wake of the WorldCom and Global Crossing cases. As the bankrupt company begins to run the reorganized company at a much lower cost, it may drive some of the remaining companies to bankruptcy due to price competition.
- Widespread mergers and acquisitions—because there are too many nonviable players with little capacity for debt service in the industry, and there is not enough business.
- Rise of the Baby Bells such as SBC, Verizon, and Bell-South. The regional and local operators stand out as bastions of stability and viability, as they own the distribution system and, therefore, have a stable customer and revenue base.

Finally, the trillion-dollar question is: Do we go back to the days of monopoly franchises because of the disaster? I hope that does not happen in light of the enormous benefits that deregulation brought to consumers. These include lower prices (long-distance), new services (cell phones), and more choices in which company to select. I think there is one area where the industry needs a great deal of help and that is how to realistically assess demand.

Footnotes

1 *Wall Street Journal,* July 22, 2002
2 *Economist,* July 20, 2002
3 *Fortune,* June 24, 2002

18

"Smart" Internet Promises Bright Future for High-Tech

Perspective: March 2004 ★

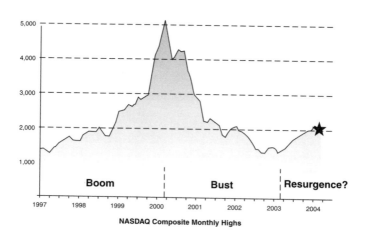

NASDAQ Composite Monthly Highs

Nearly 30 years after the invention of the Internet, it is clear that we are on the verge of reinventing it again. Undoubtedly, this is where America's competitive advantage lies. This is the real cause of my optimism about our high-tech future.

18

In the aftermath of the dot-com bust and the accompanying slide of the tech-heavy NASDAQ by more than 3,000 points from 2000 to 2003, considerable doom and gloom has prevailed about the future of high-tech and the Internet as a business technology. Such pessimism is unwarranted in light of the exciting developments in high-tech as well as growth in e-commerce.

The NASDAQ has grown steadily since last year, reflecting growing investor confidence in technology as well as e-commerce, with U.S. online sales expected to rise to more than $64 billion in 2004.

The immensity of the Internet as a business technology can be appreciated when we consider that on a worldwide basis, an estimated $3.9 trillion worth of business transactions took place over the Net in 2003. The widespread use of the Internet globally is testimony to its importance as a tool of business as well as personal convenience and service. More than 70 percent of the people in the United States, 30 percent of Chinese and 24 percent of Brazilians go online at least once a month.

The rebound in the NASDAQ is making many stock watchers nervous as they worry about a recurrence of the 2000-2003 market debacle. I think, at least at this point, such worries are unwarranted because the NASDAQ has been hovering around the 2,000 mark in 2004 and not at 5,000, as it was in 2000.

In addition, the tech companies that are doing well have learned their lessons from the boom-bust cycle about the need of having robust business plans as well as the importance of providing real value to customers.

It is not surprising that at the top of the tech food chain are mature companies such as eBay with the ideal Internet-based business model, Yahoo, Amazon.com, and Intel. The important thing is that all these companies are making money. This is a sign of maturation of our tech economy.

But the real cause of my optimism about our high-tech future is what is happening in our great research universities as well as in our leading tech companies. I will specifically focus on the Internet, since that is one of our key technologies. The promise of the Internet is going to be further enhanced as a result of recent developments in the United States.

The major advancement of the Internet lies in the work being done by a team of 100 or so top U.S. computer scientists from UC Berkeley, Princeton and MIT, who are backed by a consortium of corporate sponsors such as Hewlett-Packard, Intel and Google. The project is named PlanetLab, and the team hopes to develop a new model of the Internet that will eliminate many of its limitations by 2006.

The transformation of the current Internet system, called the "Dumb Internet," to the "Smart Internet" means the following.

- Replication of the entire workspace (programs and documents) on any Internet workstation. This will allow us laptop-less travel as long as we have access to an Internet terminal.
- Avoidance of the costly invasion of worms and viruses that disrupt our businesses as well as personal lives because the new network will destroy the

worms before they inflict damage to our computers.

- Retrieval of video and other data that use up enormous amounts of bandwidth irrespective of how many users are in the network.
- Enormous expansion of data-storage capacity that will allow secure storage of digital photos, tax returns, videos and other data for decades via the Internet. This would make hard disks, and things like storage CDs, a thing of the past.

Fundamentally, what the "Smart Internet" does is make the network the computer. In other words, it transfers data storage and computation functions from our personal computers and mainframes to the network.

One of the critical vulnerabilities of the Internet as it exists today is that the initial system was built for a small group of scientists in government and university laboratories, and as such it was built on trust. This is usually a routine assumption among scientists in major universities and think tanks.

Now the Internet has been mainstreamed with all the cultural baggage that comes with that, including destructive and highly anti-social impulses such as the transmission of worms and viruses to our Internet system that has caused billions of dollars of losses in the last few years. The "Smart Internet" has the promise of eliminating catastrophic losses and enhancing our trust in this vital technology, while making it faster, and adding enormous amounts of data and computation capacity. This will indeed be a major breakthrough.

In a few years, the "Smart Internet" will also be available for commercial and technical applications. These would include a major boost to e-commerce, making it easier for business people traveling on the road. Doctors could examine medical history from anywhere at any time, and a building contractor could fulfill a dream of modifying blueprints from home.

Nearly 30 years after the invention of the Internet in the United States, it is clear that we are on the verge of reinventing the Internet again as a result of extraordinary cooperation between business and our great research universities. Undoubtedly, this is where America's competitive advantage lies. The extraordinary collaboration between world-class research universities and leading technology companies exists in very few locations as much as it does in the Bay Area.

Who knows what exactly will be the nature of the next generation eBay or Google with the advent of the "Smart Internet." One thing I am sure about is that the chances are high that they will be incubated out of places such as the Bay Area.

Transforming good science into great technology and ultimately products and services that the world wants is how California and the United States can stay ahead of worldwide competition and maintain our high standard of living. That is the good news about the future of our economy.

III
Epilogue

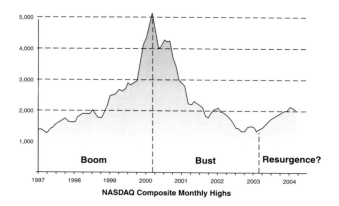

NASDAQ Composite Monthly Highs

The economy is subject
to recurrent episodes of
speculative fever, with
accompanying euphoria
followed by financial
ruin for many. There are
several significant lessons
we can learn from the
dot-com boom-to-bust
cycle and collapse of
the stock market.

Lessons Learned

The second half of the 1990s witnessed one of the most impressive periods of economic prosperity in recent history, with low unemployment, low inflation, substantial growth in real GDP, and high real wages. Many analysts, impressed with the spectacular performance of the economy, were moved to declare the end of the business cycle. The problem with the prosperity of the 1990s was that the period also coincided with one of the greatest financial bubbles in U.S. economic history. Share prices of technology, media, and telecommunication companies skyrocketed. Unreal prices had little to do with the business realities of profits and performance. Gravity-defying price-to-earnings (P/E) ratios were running into the hundreds. Amazingly enough analysts and experts were able to convince investors that these unreal ratios were actually reasonable and justifiable via the miracle of the "New Economy."

With investors' paper-wealth rising at amazing rates, individuals and businesses indulged in massive borrowing and investing, and of course, there was no need to save. The age of eternal prosperity was here. Why worry? Making lots of money was easy in the dot-com euphoria days. You could write up a business plan on the back of a napkin during lunch, get financed by a venture or angel capitalist, go on a spending binge hoping for an IPO, and then cash out. It was simple, was it not? But things really did not work out after a while as ill-conceived business plans eventually produced poor results. Ideas that were supposed to change the world went to the scrap heap of failure as hundreds of dot-coms bit the dust. The bust was here. The tech-heavy NASDAQ peaked in March 2000 and collapsed by April 2000. Billions were made and lost with the collapse of the bubble. Entrepreneurs, techies, and wide-eyed investors had a terribly rude awakening. In a matter of months accolades, praise, and arrogance were replaced by ridicule and humility.

Having critically examined the dot-com boom-bust cycle in Section II (Perspectives) of this book, what are the lessons we can learn from this roller coaster ride? There are five:

1. Hubris is Not a Substitute for a Well-developed Business Plan

Even when a business is based around a revolutionary technology, it still must have a robust business plan. A revolutionary technology such as the Internet requires as much planning and thought as a routine new technology. The euphoria surrounding new technologies can create such unrealistic financial expectations that sound economics and good business sense disappears. It is important to remember that technology is an enabler rather than an end-product in itself. It does not give us the license to mint money at will. Many of the Internet startups were not business startups at all but stock market IPO plays designed to make a fast buck. A case in point is online grocer Webvan.com, which had a poor business plan that showed the company's lack of understanding of the grocery business, a poor understanding of customer demographics, and erroneous target marketing.

2. Pay Attention to E-business Best Practices

The important principles that need to be considered in starting and sustaining e-commerce businesses are:

- Don't forget that the laws of economics are just as applicable to Internet-based businesses as they are to any traditional "Old Economy" businesses.
- Any business is fundamentally about people; technology is just a tool.
- Remember that technology changes quickly but people change slowly.
- It is essential to understand the customer, the technology, and how the customer interfaces with the technology.
- Continuously verify what the customer wants.
- Online customer service must be fast. Avoid the "world wide wait" (www) syndrome.
- Minimize delivery costs.
- Goods traded need to have a high value-to-weight ratio and cannot be perishable (e.g. books, CD's, tapes. etc.).
- Convert "mind share" to "market share" – hits on a Website must translate into cash flow.
- Location matters, even in the case of Internet-based businesses.
- Enhance employee productivity via Internet-based in-house training programs thereby moving people to higher value-added activities.
- An ideal e-business is one that follows the principles outlined above. Additionally, once it is established it has a low cost of serving and adding customers. That is a key advantage of eBay, the best e-commerce model in business.
- The recent trend of dot-com allying with brick-and-mortar companies makes good business sense. Good examples of "clicks and mortar" companies include Lands End, Toys R Us, Rite Aid, and FedEx.

- The massive spending spree to build market share, mind share, and attain a "first comer advantage" in super-speed "internet time" in the end meant huge losses for the dot-com start-ups.

3. Due Diligence is a Must

The dot-com debacle reminds us of past speculative episodes. These include the 17th century Tulip Mania in Western Europe, the 18th century South Seas Company Bubble, the crash of 1929, and the junk bond fiasco of the 1980s. The economy is subject to recurrent episodes of speculative fever, with accompanying euphoria followed by finan-cial ruin for many.

The common themes of all of these speculative manias are: a) short memory for lessons of other major financial disasters – or lack of knowledge thereof, b) promotion of un-tested business ideas by inexperienced and highly optimis-tic – and even unscrupulous people, c) unrealistic financial expectations relating to the use of new technologies or ideas due to ignorance or greed.

The unique feature of the dot-com crash was that we have seldom seen such reckless financing by venture capitalists, investment bankers, and investors. Billions of dollars were made in a matter of days. In the early stages of the dot-com mania it was possible to invest in a company, launch an IPO, and cash out before a business model could really be tested. It was the second Gold Rush in California and it fizzled out much faster than the first one. Despite the dot-com crash, where hundreds of billions of dollars were lost by starry-eyed small-time investors, many of the big time Internet gold rush prospectors cashed in their chips early in the game, and the Web made them handsomely rich.

Despite huge losses and shattered dreams it is unlikely that we will avoid future financial disasters due to greed, the thrill of being involved in a venture that promises the sky, and the opportunity to take big risks, lose it all, and then regain it all again—a reckless and dangerous sport that a market economy allows ("second chance" optimism). The only way we have to protect ourselves from falling victim to another speculative craze is continuous due diligence and a healthy does of skepticism about new-fangled things that promise untold riches.

4. Business Ethics is a Key Asset

In the past two years, we have paid a great deal of attention to the dot-com debacle. But it is shocking to realize that the telecom meltdown that has occurred since then is several magnitudes larger in its impact on the economy. The telecom meltdown was caused by highly unrealistic business expectations (building excess capacity) combined with serious lapses in corporate ethics. The impacts range from fall in equity prices, loss of jobs, erosion of retirement nest eggs, to loss of confidence in our business leadership due to serious ethical malfeasance, including fraudulent accounting.

One wonders how it is possible for American businesses to precipitate back-to-back catastrophic disasters such as the dot-com debacle and the telecom meltdown in a period of only few years. Do we have a situation where we are throwing all caution to the winds as long as we can make a big pot of money, regardless of the level of risk? Has our business value system become, "the end justifies the means"? The obvious lesson here is that sustainable business success is only possible with prudent business planning and a firm stand on good business ethics.

5. The Internet is a Technology, Not a Business Model

The final question is: Now that the bust phase of the dot-com era is behind us, where are we with respect to Internet-based commerce? The most important thing to note is that the Internet is alive and doing wonderfully. Hundreds of millions of people around the globe use it every day for e-mail, for exchange of information, as a tool of research, and most importantly, as a vehicle of education. Governments also have a Web presence in order to enhance productivity and access for the citizenry. Making money with the Internet has been difficult, but the blame for that has to be shared

Venture Capital Follows the Boom ... and Bust

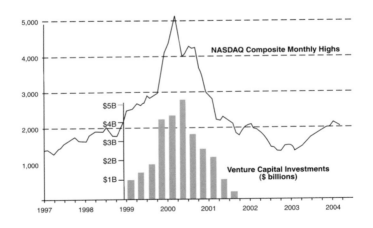

In the boom period, billions of dollars of venture capital poured into a myriad of dot-com start-ups. But once it became clear that visions of profits were no more than mirages, the money stopped flowing and companies with no other sources of financing began to fail rapidly. Source: NASDAQ, Wall Street Journal by many, including enterprise managers, venture capitalists, media, brokerage house analysts, day traders, and others. Most Internet start-ups were failures due to the incorrect assumption that the Internet itself was a business model rather than a new technology. Furthermore, the early dot-coms forgot that Internet retailing was more about retailing and less about the Internet. The "clicks-and-bricks" businesses have worked because they are using the Internet in a smart way – as one of their distribution and communication channels, but not the only one.

It has become quite clear that the best way to make money using the Internet is to bring to the customer services that would not exist without it. That is why eBay, Travelocity. com, and Expedia.com are such successes. The product they sell is "information-rich services" – and the strength of Internet lies in information.

The Internet is fast becoming a key asset in the internal operations of our businesses. Smart businesses are using it for things that only the Internet does well. Now it is gaining full legitimacy as a businesss tool in a sustainable way.

Resurgence?

In the two years since the bust of the dot-com bubble nearly 275 publicly traded dot-com businesses bit the dust - only 223 now remain alive.[1] Out of the two hundred or so surviving dot-com businesses more than 50 percent of them lost money last year.

But if one looks at the recent performance of dot-com stocks one would think that we are almost back to the "good old days" of the dot-com world. Between November 2002 and November 2003 the Dow Jones Internet Composite Index of Web based companies increased by more than 110 percent compared to an increase of about 27 percent for the Dow (Dow Jones Industrial Average) in the same period.

There are signs of investor tech euphoria emerging again nearly three years after the dot-bomb of 2000. This is worrisome. Lessons that were implicit in the aftermath of the debacle such as: a) do not buy a tech stock just because it is going up, and b) do not ignore the financials of a company, seem to have faded with rising exuberance of equity markets in 2003. Although the market as a whole did well in 2003, technology stocks took off like a rocket. A prime concern is that the NASDAQ 100 trades at nearly 100 times its 2003 earnings, compared to the S&P 500 ratio at nearly 33. The P/E ratio for Amazon at the end of 2003 was at 93 and that of Yahoo at 112.[2] It is difficult to justify these valuations. Are we justifying these unrealistic P/E ratios again using the same "New Economy" justifications prevalent in 1999, the peak of the dot-com era?

Investors who have learned the lessons of the dot-com boom-to-bomb period are now asking themselves several key questions before investing in a technology stock:

- How does the company make money?
- Are its sales real?
- How does the company compare with its competition?
- Is the company living within its means?
- Who are the leaders of the company and why are they qualified to run this business?
- Am I investing in a sound business or a good story?

What is impressive is that some of the pre-bubble dot-coms that nearly disappeared are resoundingly back again. They include Ask Jeeves, Pumatech and Rambus. Their resurgence is truly remarkable. At this time it is difficult to assess the reasons underlying these spectacular valuations in economic or financial performance terms. One hopes that these values are sustainable over the long haul. Investors need to ask the questions mentioned in the previous paragraph before buying high-flying tech stocks.

Another growing concern is that the NASDAQ poster boys of the dot-com era, the day traders, are back again in force. Day trading was up by nearly 182 percent in the first half of 2003.[3]

Finally, buying stocks on the margin is also back again in full force. Investor loans from brokers were up by 25 percent in the first half of 2003. Concerns about this trend were so high that the National Association of Securities Dealers in September 2003 warned investors that the speculative trading levels of the Dot-com era of the late 1990s were returning again. These are signs that would suggest that many of the preconditions of the dot-com to dot-bomb debacle are beginning to re-emerge. Undoubtedly this is worrisome, and we should be cautious in our investment decisions. Are we about to repeat the same mistakes again? I hope not. Let us not forget that the NASDAQ today is at around 2,000 and not at 5,000 as it was at the peak of the dot-com boom period in 2001.

There are three pieces of good news relating to business use of the Internet: 1) the emergence of the IP telephone, 2) the rise of e-commerce and the success of clicks and mortar businesses – many of them household names in the American business scene, names that would not have been associated with dot-coms just a few years ago, and 3) smart uses of the Web by well-established American businesses.

The IP Telephone

The newest excitement in the digital world involves Internet-based telephony called voice over internet protocol (VOIP). This technology digitizes voice signals then transmits voice-data packets over to the Internet network. Nearly eight years after its first introduction, VOIP today is very much front page news in the financial media. According to recent research by the Synergy Research Group,[4] the future of Internet phone systems appears to be bright: 80 percent sales growth in 2003 to $1.6 billion with projected sales of $5.3 billion by 2007.

For "techies" this means a revolution in the telecommunication business. Major VOIP related companies include Avaya, Citel Technologies, Mitel Networks, NEC, Nortel Networks, and Siemens. This may be the direction in which the telephone business is moving in the future. If that is so it will be tough on the giant telephone companies as they begin to lose market share to the latest application of the Internet – the Internet-based telephone (or IP phone). As with the wireless breakthrough, traditional phone companies may have to join the competition. The next "phone wars" are about to start. Most of the major phone companies including BellSouth, AT&T, Qwest Communications, Sprint, and Verizon are now offering IP phone options.

The advantages of the IP phone over traditional phones are many. They include: a) cost advantage; e.g. a company of 10,000 employees can reduce its long distance bill by nearly 70 percent (Forrester Research); b) reduction of the proliferation of communication gadgets such as cell phones, PDA's, small personal computers, and instant messaging. The IP phone can consolidate all these devices into a single unit. With an IP phone using unified messaging software, mobile workers can access their voice mail, e-mail, a conference call, and fax messages using an e-mail account. Another significant advantage of an IP phone system is that it does not suffer from interference which is a serious problem with cell phones.

For many businesses even these obvious advantages are not going to sway them to change to the IP system. Cost-conscious businesses are reluctant to discard their current phones systems that work quite well for most of their desk bound employees. They may switch to IP phones for employees on the go but not for majority of their workers, at least not for a while.

For investors, I think, it is another opportunity to make or lose large sums of money as they search for the hottest IP phone stocks. The rise of SpectraLink Corporation of Boulder, Colorado, serving this emerging business is a case in point. In the past year the company's stock has zoomed up an astronomical 400 percent reminding us of the heady dot-com era of the late 1990s.[5] There is a cautionary tale here.

Epilogue: Resurgence?

During the heyday of the dot-com boom in the late 90s many investors became enamored with the VOIP technology and there was great hope for the IP phone. For example, the VOIP startup Globe.com went public in 1998 and became a legend as its stock price rose by an astronomical 600 percent. Their success was short-lived – in a matter of months the company lost millions of dollars and nearly went bankrupt. It is now trying a comeback.[6] Let us hope it is a success this time. Lots of people lost a lot of money in the previous IP phone rush.

Currently the VOIP service is considered as an information service and not a telecommunication service so it is exempt from access charges. By contrast, telephone service is a source of income for state and local governments, and these revenues will suffer as VOIP makes greater inroads into the telephone market, thus regulation is likely in the near future, particularly in light of the serious fiscal problems of state and local governments. So, part of the cost advantage of VOIP companies will erode away, although it is difficult to judge by what extent.

This time I am optimistic about the chances of success for VOIP, an attractive and worthwhile technology. However, what investors need to remember is that they can lose money in companies that have promising technology with great appeal. For example, even though telephony is a vital and valuable technology, let us not forget the recent doldrums in the telecommunications market. It all depends on the price at which investors buy stock. But it may be difficult for companies to make money right away due to intense competition and startup challenges, and down-the-road regulatory pressures. There is little doubt that the VOIP technology is the wave of the future, but investors need to pick the companies very carefully if they want a VOIP play.

The Resurgence of E-Commerce

Nearly three years after the dot-com boom-to-bomb cycle it is heartening to see that a sound idea—selling things via the Internet—is alive and doing well. The results once again confirm that a good business model with sound execution and appropriate use of technology is a winner. In 2003, online commerce grew at an annual rate of 25 percent (U.S. Department of Commerce).

There is now stiff competition for the leading online retailer, Amazon.com, and the leading shopping portal, Yahoo!. It is coming from traditional bricks-and-mortar retailers. In October 2003, the world's largest retailer, Wal-Mart, rose to the 9th position as the most visited site with 10 million visits compared to 6 million in 2002. In 2002, Best Buy rose to the 12th from 14th rank. In the same period, Target's ranking improved from 17th to 11th. By contrast, Yahoo traffic dropped from 19.4 million visits in 2002 to 16.8 million visits in 2003. Microsoft MSN shopping and America On Line shopping also declined in terms of number of visits in 2003. Of course the unquestioned leader of the pack, eBay remained in 2003 with 43.8 million hits, a rise of nearly 12 million over 2002.[7]

It is important to note that traditional bricks-and-mortar retailers have their act together, and the data shows it. JCPenney's online sales were above $500 million for 2003 compared to $381 million in 2002. Wal-Mart's online sales climbed steadily through the end of 2003. Sears, the 117 year-old retailing giant, also experienced an increase in online sales of over 50 percent in 2003 over 2002.[8]

In summary, for 2003 the story is not that the old line bricks-and-mortar retailers are winning the e-commerce battle and the established dot-com e-tailers such as Amazon.com and eBay are losing. The story is that the bricks-and-mortar companies are showing that they can hold their own, serve their customers well and not lose market share.

Web-Smart Clicks-and-Mortar Companies

Without a question the surest sign that the dot-com bust is over and a Web-revival is gathering steam is the way smart businesses are using the Internet to enhance their productivity and customer service. Let us consider several recent examples of Web smart companies[9] that illustrate that the Web is hot again:

Fresh Direct, a privately owned online grocer, uses the Internet to custom make each food order at prices that are nearly 35 percent lower than its competition. The Internet not only takes the order, it sorts out 3,200 daily orders to processing areas where 600 employees prepare the various items from meat to produce. With labor costs 60 percent lower than its rivals, the company's 2003 sales were expected to be over $90 million. Remember Webvan? They had the wrong model for a online grocery store. Fresh Direct seems to have hit it right.

Wegman's, a 72-year-old food market chain, is creating a detailed online suppliers product catalog of a vast number of items that grocery stores stock. This will automate transactions between grocery suppliers and retailers. By preventing mistakes in ordering from suppliers the food retailer could be saving $1.5 million annually. Wegman's currently shares data with 100 suppliers and retailers. This has the potential of making the grocery industry a lot more efficient and well-integrated.

Dell Inc., has recently automated more of its e-commerce network by using robots on assembly lines that process orders directly from the Internet. This means that the assembly line at the Dell plant in Nashville, Tennessee, spews out 900 computers an hour instead of its previous 300 an hour. In addition to speed the new process requires only half the manpower. The company plans to Internet-automate eight other plants in the near future. At Dell, the Internet is enhancing productivity and, as a result, the company's profitability.

Kinko's, one of the best known copying/digital services company, is embarking on making its employee training program a lot more efficient by replacing 51 training sites across the U.S. for its 20,000 employees with a $2.5 million Internet-based education network (E-learning). The savings are significant - about $10 million a year. E-learning is paying off handsomely. Several months ago the company started offering services for preparing banners and signs, and stores that provide online courses on these services experienced sales increases of over 27 percent compared to 11 percent rise in stores without them. Smart use of the Internet enhances worker productivity and customer satisfaction.

BMW, the German automaker, is using the Internet to provide custom orders without sacrificing production efficiency. Buyers can design their own cars from an amazing array of 350 model variations, 500 options, 99 colors, and 170 interior trims. This option is so popular now that nearly 80 percent of car sales in Europe and 30 percent in the U.S. are custom ordered. What is most impressive about the system is that the customer obtains a specific date of delivery in a matter of seconds after entering the design options into the BMW website. BMW is a highly rated automobile company and not an Internet company. They use the Internet in a smart way.

Krispy Kreme, one of the most well known doughnut purveyors of America is using the Internet to do many important things such as tracking the doughnut mixture, putting on the right colored sprinkles, tracking managers' behavior, and avoiding excess orders. Internet-based tracking and coordination has eliminated expensive errors and raised productivity for the half a billion-dollar doughnut empire. The company's intranet (in-house Internet) reduces a lot of grunt work and allows employees to focus on a very important part of the business: customer service. This is a doughnut company, not a technology company, and they are focused on their core business.

Mattel, the well-known toy maker is using the Web to bring together toy designers from different locations to collaborate on new designs. The company has reduced the time it takes to design a product by nearly 20 percent. The design approval time is now reduced to five weeks instead of fourteen. This program is expected to raise Mattel's revenues by more than $200 million a year. It is still a toy company, but smart use of the Internet will raise revenues and offer a greater variety of toys to children in years to come.

IBM's giant intranet - the world's largest - will bring together hundreds of employees from its different locations to exchange ideas, improve skills, and collaborate on projects. This will save the company nearly $375 million in training and another $20 million a year in travel expenses. IBM now offers services to other major corporations such as Audi and Campbell Soup to set their Intranet for similar purposes – an excellent example of raising productivity, creativity, and collaboration in a vast company. Only the Internet could do this.

These examples dramatically illustrate how the Internet enhances business productivity, customer service, innovation, and management practices across a variety of businesses in the U.S. The Internet is fast becoming a key asset in the internal operations of our businesses. The important thing to note is that all these companies are smart about using the Internet. They are using it for things that only the Internet does well. The Internet actually never went away. It just got a bad name because of the dot-com debacle. Now it is gaining full legitimacy as a valuable tool in business and in our personal and civic lives. The Internet is back in the business world, but in a more sustainable way.

The best sign of the revival of Internet-related businesses is the comeback of several ex dot-comers in Silicon Valley who had become overnight millionaires via boom-time winnings. They are now using their own money to seed startups in Silicon Valley. They are motivated by not just the possibility of making more money but seem to be very interested in fully realizing the potential of the Internet that was derailed because of the excesses of the dot-com bubble.[10] These young veterans who made good in the dot-com mania are wise, and they are making sure that buzzwords do not replace business fundamentals. Their business philosophy is to first find out what the customers want and then create something that fulfills these needs.

Both investors and entrepreneurs can benefit as they reflect on these lessons from the dot-com boom-to-bomb phenomenon. The euphoria and mania that we saw in the high-flying dot-com boom years can be replaced by well-reasoned use of the Internet. Just as the Internet has matured over the past several years, so have we.

Epilogue: Resurgence?

Footnotes

1 *Wall Street Journal*, December 1, 2003, p. A1
2 *Business 2.0*, Nov. 2003, p. 100
3 Ibid.
4 *Time*, Bonus Section, Inside Business, January 2004
5 *Wall Street Journal*, November 13, 2003, p. C1
6 *Wall Street Journal*, December 1, 2003, p. 1
7 Bambi Francisco, CBS MarketWatch.com, *e-Newsletter*, December 1, 2003
8 *Business Week*, November 24, 2003
9 Bambi Francisco, op. cit.
10 *Forbes*, December 22, 2003

Bibliography

Allbriton, Chris. *"The Future of the Web? Two Men's Paths Tell Tale."* Contra Costa Times, January 4,1998, D8.

Barabasi, Albert-Laszlo. Linked: *How Everything Is Connected to Everything Else and What It Means for Business, Science, and Everyday Life.* New York, N.Y.: Plume, 2003.

Barlow, John Perry. *"The Economy of Ideas."* Wired, March 1994, 85. (On-line), 17 pages. Available: http://www.hotwired.com/wired/2.03/features/economy.ideas.html.

Bolt, David, and Ray Crawford. *Digital Divide: Computers and Our Children's Future.* New York, N.Y.: TV Books, 2000.

Brandenburger, Adam M., and Bary J. Nalebuff. *Co-opetition.* New York: Doubleday, 1996.

Brenner, Robert. *The Boom and The Bubble: The U.S. in the World Economy.* New York, N.Y.: Verso, 2002.

Brynjolfsson, Erik, and Brian Kahin. *Understanding the Digital Economy: Data, Tools, and Research.* Cambridge, Massachusetts and London, England: The MIT Press, 2000.

Carton, Sean. *The Dot.Bomb Survival Guide: Surviving and Thriving in the Dot.Com Implosion.* New York, N.Y.: McGraw-Hill, 2002.

Cassidy, John. *Dot.Con: The Greatest Story Ever Sold.* New York, N.Y.: HarperCollins Publishers, 2002.

Cortese, Amy. *"Computer Associates: Sexy? No. Profitable? You Bet."* Business Week, 11 November 1996.

Davis, Stan, and Christopher Meyer. *Blur: The Speed of Change in the Connected Economy.* Reading, MA.: Addison-Wesley, 1998.

Dyson, Esther. *Release 2.0: A Design for Living in the Digital Age.* New York, N.Y.: Broadway Books, 1997.

Evans, Philip, and Thomas S. Wurster. *Blown to Bits: How the New Economics of Information Transforms Strategy.* Boston, MA.: Harvard Business School of Press, 2000.

Friedlander, Amy. *Emerging Infrastructure: The Growth of Railroads.* Arlington, VA.: CNRI, 1995(a).

_____. *Natural Monopoly and Universal Service: Telephones and Telegraphs in the U.S. Communications Infrastructure.* Arlington, VA.: CNRI, 1996.

Galbraith, John Kenneth. *A Short History of Financial Euphoria.* USA: Whittle Direct Books, 1990.

Gatlin, Jonathan. *Bill Gates: The Path to the Future.* New York, N.Y.: Avon Books Inc, 1999.

Gilbert, Richard. *"Networks, Standards, and the Use of the Market Dominance: Microsoft 1995"* in *The Antitrust Revolution: Economics, Competition, and Policy,* edited by John Kwoka and Laurence White (New York: Oxford University Press, 1998).

Goldstein, Jon. *"Michael Bloomberg's Wired World."* Time Digital, 23 March 1998, 64-67.

Grove, Andrew S. *Only the Paranoid Survive: How to Exploit the Crisis Points That Challenge Every Company and Career.* New York, N.Y.: Currency Doubleday, 1996.

Hayes, John R. *"Acquisition Is Fine, But Organic Growth Is Better."* Forbes, 30 December 1996, 52-56.

James, Geoffrey. *Success Secrets From Silicon Valley: How to Make Your Teams More Effective.* New York: Times Books, 1996.

Kanter, Rosabeth Moss. *Evolve! Succeeding in the Digital Culture of Tomorrow.* Boston, MA.: Harvard Business School Press, 2001.

Kelly, Kevin. *New Rules for the New Economy: 10 Radical Strategies for a Connected World.* New York: Viking, 1998.

Kindleberger, Charles P. *Manias, Panics, and Crashes: A History of Financial Crises.* USA: John Wiley & Sons Inc., 2000.

Knight, Charles. *The Old Printer and the Modern Press.* London: John Murray, 1854.

Krugman, Paul. *The Great Unraveling: Losing Our Way in the New Century.* New York: W.W. Norton & Company, 2003.

Kuo, David J. *Dot.bomb: My Days and Nights at an Internet Goliath.* New York: Little, Brown and Company, 2001.

Lesk, Michael. *"Projections for Making Money on the Web"* in Deborah Hurley, Brian Kahin, and Hal R. Varian, eds., *Internet Publishing and*

Bibliography

Beyond. Cambridge: MIT Press, 1998.

Lewis, T. G. *The Friction-Free Economy: Marketing Strategies for a Wired World.* New York, N.Y.: HarperCollins Publishers, 1997.

Lucky, Robert. *Silicon Dreams: Information, Man, and Machine.* New York: St. Martin's Press, 1989.

Mackay, Charles. *Extraordinary Popular Delusions the Madness of Crowds.* New York: Crown Trade Paperbacks, 1980.

Magretta, Joan. *Managing in the New Economy.* Boston, MA.: Harvard Business Review Book, 1999.

Mandel, Michael. *The High-Risk Society: Peril and Promise in the New Economy.* New York: Time Business, 1996.

Martin, Chuck. *Net Future: The 7 Cybertrends That Will Drive Your Business, Create New Wealth, and Define Your Future.* New York: McGraw-Hill, 1999.

Martin, James. *Cybercorp: The New Business Revolution.* New York: Amacom, 1996.

Middleton, John. *Writing the New Economy.* Milford, CT: Capstone Publishing, 2000.

Murray, Alan. *The Wealth of Choices: How the New Economy Puts Power in Your Hands and Money in Your Pocket.* New York: Crown Business, 2000.

Papows, Jeff. *Enterprise.com: Market Leadership in the Information Age.* Reading, MA.: Perseus Books, 1998.

Perkins, Anthony B., and Michael C. Perkins. *The Internet Bubble: Inside the Overvalued World of High-Tech Stocks and What You Need to Know to Avoid The Coming Shakeout.* New York: HarperBusiness, 1999.

Rajan, Raghuram G., and Luigi Zingales. *Saving Capitalism From the Capitalists: Unleashing the Power of Financial Markets to Create Wealth and Spread Opportunity.* New York: Crown Business, 2003.

Schiller, Herbert I. *Information Inequality: The Deepening Social Crisis in America.* New York: Routledge, 1996.

Schwartz, Evan I. *Webonomics: Nine Essential Principles for Growing Your Business on the World Wide Web.* New York: Broadway Books, 1997.

Shapiro, Carl, and Hal R. Varian. *Information Rules: A Strategic Guide to the Network Economy.* Boston, MA.: Harvard Business School Press, 1999.

Shiller, Robert J. *Irrational Exuberance*. Princeton, NJ.: Princeton University Press, 2000.

_____. *The New Financial Order: Risk in the 21st Century*. Princeton, NJ.: Princeton University Press, 2003.

Siebel, Thomas M., and Pat House. *Cyber Rules: Strategies for Excelling at E-Business*. New York: Currency Doubleday, 1999.

Southwick, Karen. *Silicon Gold Rush: The New Generation of High-Tech Stars Rewrites the Rules of Business*. New York: John Wiley & Sons, Inc., 1999.

Stiglitz, Joseph E. *The Roaring Nineties: A New History of the World's Most Prosperous Decade*. New York: W. W. Norton & Company, 2003.

Tapscott, Don, Alex Lowy, and David Ticoll. *Blueprint to the Digital Economy: Creating Wealth in the Era of E-Business*. New York: McGraw-Hill, 1998.

_____. *Digital Capital: Harnessing the Power of Business Webs*. Boston, MA.: Harvard Business School Press, 2000.

_____. *Growing up Digital: The Rise of the Net Generation*. New York: McGraw-Hill, 1998.

_____. *The Digital Economy: Promise and Peril in the Age of Networked Intelligence*. New York: McGraw-Hill, 1996.

Thurow, Lester. *Fortune Favors the Bold: What We Must do to Build a New and Lasting Global Prosperity*. New York: HarperCollins Publishers, 2003.

Varian, Hal R. *"Pricing Information Goods"* in Research Libraries Group, ed., *Scholarship of the New Information Environment Proceedings*. Washington, D.C.: Research Libraries Group, 1995.

Watt, Ian. *The Rise of the Novel*. Berkeley: University of California Press, 1957.

Wingfield, Nick. *"Microsoft Says It Will Buy E-Mail Start-Up in Stock Deal"* Wall Street Journal, 1998.

Winkler, Karen. *"Academic Presses Look to the Internet to Save Scholarly Monographs,"* in *The Chronicle of Higher Education*, 12 September 1997.

Ziegler, Bart and Don Clark. *"Microsoft Gives Technology Away to Beat Rival."* Wall Street Journal, 2 October 1996. B1.

Tapan Munroe, Ph.D.

Tapan Munroe is well-known in California and the U.S. for his consulting and advisory work. His areas of expertise include regional economics, utility and energy economics, economic development, macroeconomic analysis, and strategic planning. In 2003, Tapan joined the Capital Corporation of the West (CCOW), a bank holding company in California's Central Valley, as its Chief Economist. Prior to joining CCOW, Tapan served as Chief Economist for the Pacific Gas & Electric Company. He also heads his own economic consulting firm, Munroe Consulting Inc.

Tapan received his Ph.D. in Economics from the University of Colorado. He is also a graduate of the Executive Training Program of the University of Chicago. Tapan began his teaching career as a professor at the University of the Pacific in Stockton, California, and later became Chair of the Department of Economics. He has been a visiting scholar at the Massachusetts Institute of Technology, the University of Augsburg in West Germany, and Stanford University. He was also an adjunct professor of economics at the University of California, Berkeley.

Tapan has received numerous awards and honors including the University of Colorado fellowship and membership in Phi Kappa Phi and Omicron Delta Epsilon. He was a Senior Fellow of the Great Valley Center, Modesto, California, and held the Kiriyama Distinguished

Professorship for Asia Pacific Studies at the University of San Francisco for 1998-99.

Tapan is currently a Foundation Trustee of the University of California at Merced, a member of the University of California President's Board on Science & Innovation, and on the Board of Directors of the Center for Pacific Rim Studies at the University of San Francisco. He has served as the President of the National Association of Business Economists (Bay Area chapter), past Chair of the Economics Committee, Edison Electric Institute (Washington, D.C.), quarterly Chair of the Commonwealth Club of California, and member of the National Petroleum Council Task Force on Oil Prices.

A widely published author and a nationally known speaker, Tapan Munroe has been a frequent commentator on regional and national radio and TV news programs including KRON TV (Channel 4), KGO TV (Channel 7), CNBC (Los Angeles and New York), Dow Jones Investors Network (NY) and Bloomberg News Service (NY).

Tapan has been a columnist on economic issues for the *San Francisco Examiner* and for *The Journal of Corporate Renewal.* His *Global Village* column is published bi-weekly by the *Contra Costa Times* (Knight Ridder Newspapers). His other books include *Economic Imperialism* (with Kenneth Boulding, University of Michigan Press), and *Public Power in California* (with Ted Bradshaw and Richard Lee, Xlibris Inc.).

Notes

Notes

Notes

Notes

Notes